Are you hurting? Pray. Do you feel great? Sing. Are you sick? Call the church leaders together to pray and anoint you with oil in the name of the Master. Believing-prayer will heal you, and Jesus will put you on your feet. And if you've sinned, you'll be forgiven – healed inside and out.

**James 5:13-15 (MSG)**

# OUR Lenten PRAYER

Reflections and Observations
from The Lord's Prayer

A Lenten Study
## by Olu Brown

Market
Square
BOOKS

# Our Lenten Prayer

*Reflections and Observations from The Lord's Prayer*

©2021 Olu Brown, dba Culverhouse LLC

books@marketsquarebooks.com
P.O. Box 23664  Knoxville, Tennessee 37933

ISBN: 978-1-950899-47-0

Printed and Bound in the United States of America
Cover Illustration & Book Design ©2020 Market Square Publishing, LLC

Editor: Sheri Carder Hood
Post-Process Editor: Ken Rochelle

## Scripture quotations taken from the
## New Revised Standar Version Bibe unless noted otherwise:

# Table of Contents

# INTRODUCTION
## The Season of Lent

Lent is a special season of the year during which we reflect on our lives and our relationship with Christ, earnestly repent of our sins, and grow purposefully in our faith and relationship with God. It is special because it marks the season on the liturgical calendar for Christian Churches around the world, just before Holy Week and Easter. We know Easter to be the pinnacle of the Christian calendar, and Lent is the season that prepares us for the celebration and victory of Jesus' resurrection from the grave on Easter.

> *Lent is a season of forty days, not counting Sundays, which begins on Ash Wednesday and ends on Holy Saturday. "Lent" comes from the Anglo-Saxon word "lencten," which means "spring.*[1]

During Lent, worshipers around the world join together in a common theme of our Christian faith and practice self reflection and remembrance of the sacrifice Jesus Christ made on Calvary. It is not only a

---

1 *The United Methodist Book of Worship.* "Lent" (Nashville: The United Methodist Publishing House, 1992), 320.

time of individual reflection, but a time of communal reflection, reminding us that we are a global community of believers, and we have a responsibility to one another and to our world. One prayer during Lent that calls for reflection, repentance, and accountability is this:

> *O Lord our God, teach us temperance and*
> *  self-control,*
> *That we may live in the Spirit*
> *And be mindful of all that Jesus endured and*
> *  sacrificed for our sakes,*
> *And how he was made perfect through sufferings.*
> *Help us so to keep the fast that you have chosen,*
> * That we may loose the bonds of wickedness,*
> *Undo the heavy burdens, and let the oppressed*
> *  go free;*
> *Through the grace of Christ Jesus our crucified*
> *  and risen Savior. Amen.*[2]

The phrase, "Let the oppressed go free," rings in our ears as we see the oppression in our world up close and far away, those who are oppressed physically, mentally, emotionally, and spiritually. Like Christ, we are called to help set the oppressed free. Lent is a very powerful time of year when the chains of bondage that have captured and held us in places of sin, anger, unforgiveness, apathy, and greed must be loosed, and we are set free into a new life in Jesus Christ.

---

[2] *The United Methodist Book of Worship.* "Lent" (Nashville: The United Methodist Publishing House, 1992), 337.

Lent is also a time when many of us practice spiritual disciplines to help us intentionally set our focus on God and our discipleship as a follower of Jesus Christ, disciplines such as:

- Fasting
- Meditation
- Study
- Surrender (Trust in God)
- Generosity
- Service
- Simplicity
- Quietness

During Lent, there are popular fasts like the *Daniel Fast,* which encourages people to eat only vegetables as Daniel did when he was in King Nebuchadnezzar of Babylon's court:

> *But Daniel resolved that he would not defile himself with the royal rations of food and wine; so he asked the palace master to allow him not to defile himself.*
>
> **Daniel 1:8 (NRSV)**

I was introduced to the *Daniel Fast* when I served as an associate pastor at a local church and was truly amazed to see the dedication of God's people to fasting and practicing this treasured spiritual discipline. I

3

saw lives transformed through fasting and taking time to seek God's will and direction for their lives, which inspired others to observe fasting during Lent.

There are also Lenten challenges that encourage us to abstain from social media and other forms of entertainment and activities that may distract us from our relationship with God. I believe fasting from social media may be much more difficult today than adjusting our diet because social media and our smart phones have become such an integral part of our everyday lives. There are those who could not imagine a single hour without checking their social media or scrolling through their smartphones.

In a social media statistics report by the Pew Research Center subtitled, *How often Americans use social media sites,* the research revealed:

> **For many users, social media is part of their daily routine. Seven-in-ten Facebook users – and around six-in-ten Instagram and Snapchat users – visit these sites at least once a day.**[3]

This research is not surprising because this is an area of tension for a lot of people who really want to spend more quality time with God and others, but are caught between interacting with people on their smartphones and social media platforms versus spending

---

[3] "Social Media Fact Sheet," https://www.pewresearch.org/internet/fact-sheet/social-media/, April 2021.

> **Many of us lapse into old, familiar ways, even after making New Year's resolutions.**

time in solitude, meditation, prayer with God and actual in-person conversations with others. It is not uncommon to have a bit of trepidation when considering fasting from technology during Lent.

Lent provides a time for us to recalibrate shortly after the new calendar year and ask reflective questions: Who am I? What consumes my life? Am I living in default mode or with purpose-filled intention?

Many of us lapse into old, familiar ways, even after making New Year's resolutions and setting lofty personal goals for progressive changes. With little intentionality or daily direction, we often forget to seek God's guidance so that we may achieve God's higher calling and purpose for our lives. Lent offers a season for us to reset – even dismantle – our default button and dare to live in God's direction and plan for our lives, fully surrendering to God's purpose.

This Lent, I hope you choose to reset and allow God to speak into your life in fresh ways so that you can see with new eyes, hear with new ears, and discern with a new heart.

How might we do this? One of my favorite scriptures answers this question:

*Trust in the Lord with all your heart;*
*don't rely on your own intelligence.*

**Proverbs 3:5 (CEB)**

During this Lenten season, I encourage you to lean fully on God and practice the spiritual discipline of trust. There is so much we don't know or understand, and so much we have to learn. In my daily conversations, I continue to be reminded that the world is greater than I can imagine, and the future will always be unknown. To attempt to be God, knowing all of the geography of the world and the future is a futile exercise that, at the end of the day, will leave me feeling disappointed and disillusioned.

Perhaps God is challenging us to fully release and trust God for all things in our lives during this Lenten season. It doesn't mean we literally stop and cease to do anything, but we live and operate with the mindset that God is in control and has our best interests at heart even when we don't fully understand what God is doing or perceive God's presence in our lives and world. We need to be open and willing to ask God for help and direction.

God is available to lead and guide us every step of the way. I know this Lent will be remarkable as we travel toward Easter together and choose to live life with intentional purpose.

6

## The Spiritual Discipline of Trust

The spiritual discipline of trust is best activated through prayer – which is the subject of this Lenten study – specifically the Lord's Prayer, found in the Gospel of Matthew, Chapter 6. I look forward to taking this prayer journey and trusting God together as God leads us to a greater purpose for our lives than we could ever imagine.

The season of Lent begins on Ash Wednesday. On this day, churches around the world host their Ash Wednesday worship experiences, a communal gathering with song, prayer, and a homily that ends with the impartation of ashes as a priest, pastor, or layperson places actual ashes on the forehead of each congregant.

On Ash Wednesday, we are called to reflect on the brevity of life: "Remember that you are dust, and to dust, you shall return. Repent, and believe the gospel."[4]

COVID-19 shifted and changed everything. The pandemic forced churches to think differently about sharing in the liturgical seasons with parishioners who were used to attending places of worship and traditionally engaging in the church calendar. In Atlanta, our church offered a creative solution to Ash Wednesday by hosting a drive-through opportunity,

---

[4] *The United Methodist Book of Worship.* "Lent" (Nashville: The United Methodist Publishing House, 1992), 323.

allowing parishioners to drive to the church and receive ashes under one of four makeshift tents located in the parking lot. There was music playing in the background, and each of our clergy members was at a tent station imparting ashes through open car windows or to people walking up to one of the stations. The weather was beautiful and God's grace was present. What could have been a season of loss was reclaimed as a season of hope for God's people. It was a meaningful, poignant experience that gave parishioners tradition and innovation at the same time.

The duration of Lent is forty days, excluding Sundays, which are thought to be mini-Easter events. Lent ends during Holy Week, leading up to Easter.

The number forty is not uncommon in the Biblical text, and there are many references to forty days.

- In Exodus 24, Moses was on Mt. Sinai for forty days and forty nights and received God's law and Ten Commandments.

- During a revival in Nineveh, Jonah prophesied: "Forty days more, and Nineveh shall be overthrown!" And the people of Nineveh believed God; they proclaimed a fast, and everyone, great and small, put on sackcloth" (Jonah 3:4-5 NRSV).

- Jesus fasted in the wilderness for forty days and forty nights: "Then Jesus was led up by the Spirit into the wilderness to be tempted by the devil. He fasted forty days and forty nights, and afterward, he was famished" (Matthew 4:1-2 NRSV).

Jesus was alone – fasting, tested, and tempted in the wilderness – yet he overcame every temptation and hardship. During our forty days of Lent, we can more closely identify with Jesus' wilderness experience because we are in the midst of transition, fasting, testing, tempting, and receiving new revelation about God and ourselves.

Like Christ, we are preparing for Calvary, the cross, and the celebration of Easter. Our forty-day Lenten journey will be like none other as we open ourselves to the glory and mystery of God at work in our lives, even in the middle of the wilderness.

Holy Week in the Protestant Christian church typically consists of Palm Sunday, Maundy Thursday, Good Friday, and Easter Sunday, with Lent ending just before Easter.

During Lent and Holy Week, we believers will spend time focusing on our personal relationship with God through Jesus Christ and reflect introspectively on the condition of our souls. We will also focus on our relationships with ourselves and with our brothers and sisters. We will examine how we are showing up in the world and explore whether we live life intentionally with purpose or live on default. Reflecting on these thoughts

is challenging because it takes us deep within our being
and shows us how we are with ourselves and how we
present ourselves to others and God.

Do you ever wonder what Jesus wrestled
with during his forty days and forty nights in the
wilderness? Do you think about the prayers he prayed,
and the thoughts he pondered? The wilderness was a
necessary and unavoidable time that was a precursor
to Jesus' public ministry. During Lent, like Jesus,
you may feel you are in a wilderness season. My
encouragement to you is to hold on and know that, even
in the wilderness of life, you are not alone and God has
not forgotten about you.

Lent is our spiritual wilderness where and when
we can find clarity to some of life's questions and
emerge stronger, wiser, and better equipped to manage
the world's cares. During Lent, we are called away
from the world's distractions to reflect and discern
who God is and who we are. Lent is a bit of a retreat
and refuge during a time of year when everyone and
everything seems to run on a fast autopilot setting. If
we never stop to reset and rethink, we will go another
365 days the same way we did the previous 365 days,
and eventually, the years add up to decades, and the
decades add up to a lifetime.

I hope you will consciously take your life off the
default autopilot setting and fully live and experience

life this Lent. There will be times when living will be painful because God will reveal truths about you and others that are unsettling in your wilderness. There will be times when you survey the state of the world, and your hope may be challenged. But beyond the difficulties, you will be renewed and refreshed with a new perspective on life and the world. At the end of Jesus' wilderness experience, scripture says, "Then the devil left him, and suddenly angels came and waited on him" (Matthew 4:11 NRSV).

You need to know that you are not going through Lent alone because a community of believers is journeying and believing with you. Like you, they seek a closer relationship with God on their journeys and to be more in tune with themselves and the world in which they live. They have high hopes for discernment and clarity and wish to emerge from Lent stronger and wiser. The angels attended to Jesus in his wilderness, and the angels are attending to you today in your Lenten experience.

As you journey through the season of Lent, God will transform you. I remember Lent seasons in the past when I didn't completely embrace the season or wholeheartedly participate in the spiritual disciplines, especially fasting. Admittedly, I thought some of the spiritual practices during Lent were something people did out of tradition, not transformation. Tradition is when we go through religious routines simply to check off a list with boxes so we can to say publicly that we achieve a certain goal.

I believe this was the very practice Jesus warned against in Matthew 6. If we are not careful, we can get tradition confused with transformation and think that a series of rote ritual practices is actual transformation, but it is not. Transformation is the exact opposite of tradition, although one can be transformed by traditional practices in the life of the church such as fasting, prayer, Holy Communion, and meditation.

Transformation is more about the mindset when we live out the spiritual practices knowing that there is nothing we can do to cause God to love us any more or less than God already loves us. When we live out the spiritual disciplines of the Church, we do it out of our gratitude for God's grace and our desire to be in right relationship with God.

Over the years, though, I have come to experience the power of transformation during Lent and the importance of yielding my whole self to the work of the Holy Spirit during the season. I have shifted from practicing the tradition of religion to fully yielding myself to God's work in my life to transform my mind and my heart during the Lenten season, and it has made all of the difference. Whenever we fully surrender to God during Lent, the spiritual disciplines are a means, not an end.

Because prayer is a transformative spiritual

discipline, the backdrop of this Lenten study is the most famous prayer of all time, the Lord's Prayer from Matthew's Gospel:

> *And whenever you pray, do not be like the hypocrites; for they love to stand and pray in the synagogues and at the street corners, so that they may be seen by others. Truly I tell you, they have received their reward. But whenever you pray, go into your room and shut the door and pray to your Father who is in secret; and your Father who sees in secret will reward you.*
>
> *When you are praying, do not heap up empty phrases as the Gentiles do; for they think that they will be heard because of their many words. Do not be like them, for your Father knows what you need before you ask him. Pray then in this way:*
>
> > *Our Father in Heaven,*
> > *hallowed be your name.*
> > *Your kingdom come.*
> > *Your will be done,*
> > *on Earth as it is in Heaven.*
> > *Give us this day our daily bread.*
> > *And forgive us our debts,*
> > *as we also have forgiven our debtors.*
> > *And do not bring us to the time of trial,*
> > *but rescue us from the evil one.*
>
> **Matthew 6:5-13 (NRSV)**

This historic Lord's Prayer is a spiritual discipline and sacred literature that has survived the ages and helped generations connect more deeply with God and community. This Lent, I ask you to walk with me through the words of the Lord's Prayer and consider making this prayer a daily part of your spiritual focus. You may choose to pray the entire prayer once a day or multiple times a day. You may wish to focus on a different word, phrase, or verse each day and combine it with the spiritual discipline of meditation.

I encourage you to treat this 40-day Lenten journey as a marathon, not a sprint. However you choose to engage the Lord's Prayer this Lent, it will be the best way for you, and the end result will be a closer relationship with God and the community of people in your life. Thank you for taking this soul-searching journey with me. Together we can clear the path toward Easter.

# Questions

What is an issue or problem on your mind as you begin this Lenten season?

How does reading (or hearing) the Lord's Prayer make you feel?

# CHAPTER ONE
## Jesus' Model Prayer

*I am no longer my own, but thine.*
*Put me to what thou wilt, rank me with whom thou wilt.*
*Put me to doing, put me to suffering.*
*Let me be employed by thee or laid aside for thee,*
*exalted for thee or brought low for thee.*
*Let me be full, let me be empty.*
*Let me have all things, let me have nothing.*
*I freely and heartily yield all things*
*to thy pleasure and disposal.*
*And now, O glorious and blessed God,*
*Father, Son, and Holy Spirit,*
*thou art mine, and I am thine. So be it.*
*And the covenant which I have made on earth,*
*let it be ratified in heaven. Amen.*[5]

One of the most meaningful ways to experience Lent is through prayer. One year I subscribed to Mark Batterson's 40 Day Prayer Challenge based on his book, *The Circle Maker,* which focuses on strategic and purposeful prayer. Batterson is a leading voice in the Protestant Church worldwide, a successful church planter, author, and prayer warrior. In the companion

---

[5]  Discipleship Ministries, *The Wesley Covenant Prayer.* https://www.umcdiscipleship.org/blog/the-wesley-covenant-prayer-and-the-baptismal-covenant. Accessed November 1, 2021.

forty-day prayer devotion book, he said the following about God, life, and prayer:

*If you want God to do something new in you, you cannot keep doing the same old thing. You must do something different. And if you do, God will create new capacities within you. There will be new gifts and new revelations. But you've got to pray the price. You'll get out of this what you put into it.* [6]

What Batterson said about doing "something different" is essential. If we aren't careful, we can mindlessly participate year after year in the church, celebrating the seasons out of rote memory. Without consciously and completely surrendering to God, we likely miss the power and fresh revelation God has in store for us in this moment and year.

My hope for you this Lent is that you do prayer differently and allow God to speak to you profoundly through the Lord's Prayer. Like Mark Batterson said, "God will create new capacities within you."

You have the opportunity to grow and develop in fresh ways, and although at times it won't be easy or comfortable, you will be growing and evolving into a disciple of Jesus Christ and sharing the love of Christ with the world. Do not settle for Lent or prayer, as usual, this time. Instead, trust God to lead you and to

---

[6] Mark Batterson. *Draw the Circle: The 40 Day Prayer Challenge* (Zondervan. Grand Rapids, Michigan: Zondervan, 2012), 8.

illuminate the Lord's Prayer in a way that gives you a fresh revelation for your life and community.

Jesus' approach was often antithetical to the culture and norms of his time. While giving a counter-cultural sermon on a mountainside over two thousand years ago, Jesus delivered words of wisdom that will last throughout eternity. These profound words, contained within the Sermon on the Mount, are called the Beatitudes.

> *When Jesus saw the crowds, he went up the mountain; and after he sat down, his disciples came to him. Then he began to speak and taught them, saying:*
> *"Blessed are the poor in spirit, for theirs is the kingdom of Heaven.*
> *"Blessed are those who mourn, for they will be comforted.*
> *"Blessed are the meek, for they will inherit the Earth.*
> *"Blessed are those who hunger and thirst for righteousness, for they will be filled.*
> *"Blessed are the merciful, for they will receive mercy.*
> *"Blessed are the pure in heart, for they will see God.*
> *"Blessed are the peacemakers, for they will be called children of God.*
> *"Blessed are those who are persecuted for righteousness' sake, for theirs is the kingdom of Heaven.*

> *"Blessed are you when people revile you and*
> *persecute you and utter all kinds of evil against*
> *you falsely on my account.*
> *Rejoice and be glad, for your reward is great in*
> *Heaven, for in the same way they persecuted the*
> *prophets who were before you."*
>
> **Matthew 5:1-12 (NRSV)**

These remarkable words reiterate the phrase, "Blessed are the..." and challenge the reader and listener to think more deeply, love others more generously, and live with moral integrity and accountability to God and the world.

In the Sermon on the Mount, Jesus also reflects on salt, light, marriage, love, and murder in ways that give the listeners a new archetype for thinking and living out critical aspects of the human condition. Jesus' sermons were radical and relevant, and they often went against the culture of his day – as they do even now – and collided with conventional theology and wisdom. The Sermon on the Mount both inspires and challenges simultaneously, directing the listener and the would-be disciple to a higher calling and level of living.

The Sermon on the Mount was – and is – relevant because its content represented real-life occurrences in the communities during Jesus' earthly journey. He was not afraid to use the proclamation moment as an opportunity to address the concerns and issues that cut to the core of philosophy and theology. No more radical words could Jesus preach than to say:

> *Blessed are the poor in spirit, for theirs is the kingdom of heaven. Blessed are those who mourn, for they will be comforted. Blessed are the meek, for they will inherit the earth.*
>
> **5:3-5 (NRSV)**

To publicly say that the poor, the grieving, and the meek held keys to the kingdom of Heaven, would be comforted, and inherit the Earth was radical preaching and a direct challenge to those in power and authority to say that God's way does not necessarily align with the ways of the world. In God's economy and kingdom, "So the last will be first, and the first will be last" (Matthew 20:16 NRSV).

In the middle of Jesus' sermon, he pivots to prayer and offers instructions and content on how his disciples should pray. This prayer is what we refer to as the Lord's Prayer.

I know people who have attended conferences, watched media and spent countless hours with preachers, spiritual guides, and mentors learning about prayer. I am sure each of these experiences had merit and yielded results. Still, there could be no greater rabbi (teacher) than Jesus and no more remarkable experience than being able to sit at Jesus' feet as he gave his disciples instructions on how to communicate with their Creator. The poignant instructions he shared over two thousand years ago are still relevant for us today. And the wonderful blessing is, if we follow these instructions, we too will be sitting at the feet of our Savior learning how to communicate with our Creator.

The Lord's Prayer has been taught and recited throughout the generations before children fall asleep, around dinner tables, before deliberations and decisions begin in meetings, and during large public gatherings where the attendees are prompted with two words: "Our Father." And, like a choir, participants join their voices together in a resounding chorus. I have experienced this beautiful chorus at the graveside committals of lives once lived, where we conclude with the language of the committal:

> *This body we commit to the ground*
> *Earth to earth, ashes to ashes, dust to dust.*
> *Blessed are the dead who die in the Lord.*
> *Yes, says the Spirit, they will rest from*
> *their labors for their deeds follow them.*[7]

The committal language then ends with the recommendation in italics, *The Lord's Prayer may follow.* In each of the committal services I have officiated, I

---

[7] *The United Methodist Book of Worship.* "A Service of Committal" (Nashville: The United Methodist Publishing House, 1992), 155-157.

always end with the Lord's Prayer, and without fail, the congregation joins together in one resounding voice.

Part of the genius of Jesus' micro-sermon on prayer was to remind listeners to be mindful of how one prays. In Matthew 6:5, Jesus states, "When you pray, do not be like…." There was a deep and abiding concern that the prayer life of a disciple should not be flashy and boastful, but rather, one that is humble and personal. Jesus demonstrated this type of modest, private prayer life. In the Gospels, Jesus slipped away to pray alone. Hence, it was not out of the norm for Jesus to recommend to his disciples that their prayer lives be meaningful and focused on their relationship with God, not based on a desire to perform and be heard and seen in the public domain.

In a sense, Jesus was encouraging his disciples to take a minimalist, simplistic approach to their prayer lives – not in the format of minimal content and superficial conversation but less about sequencing long, drawn-out words attempting to impress God and bystanders with perfectly articulated vocabulary and oratory skills.

In our society, there is so much commentary about simple, simplistic living. Some refer to this as a "minimalist lifestyle approach." There are do-it-yourself reality TV shows on building and living in "tiny homes" where residents downsize from two to three thousand square feet to less than five hundred square feet. Interior design magazines and online resources showcase rooms, homes, and offices with a simple, streamlined, clutter-free design approach to colors, art, and furnishings. One article defines *minimalist interior design* in this way:

> *Minimalist interior design is very similar to modern interior design and involves using the bare essentials to create a simple and uncluttered space. It's characterized by simplicity, clean lines, and a monochromatic palette with colour used as an accent. It usually combines an open floor plan, lots of light, and functional furniture, and it focuses on the shape, colour and texture of just a handful of essential elements.* [8]

To apply this interior design concept to Jesus' teaching on prayer, we are called to have a "bare essential," "simple and uncluttered" approach to prayer, a process that leaves us fully available to hear and receive God's words and will for our lives. This is good news for people like me who struggle with prayer and think that our prayers have to be filled with eloquent words and phrases that cause listeners to tune in and believe we have a special communication with God. The truth is that we all have a direct communication line with God and God is not impressed with our words and phrases but rather deeply desires that we communicate. However the words come out, it is okay with God.

---

[8] What is minimalist interior design style? Tarkett 2021. https://home.tarkett.com/en_EU/node/what-is-minimalist-interior-design-style-8860.

This style of prayer does not sacrifice content but focuses less on presentation and more on how we show up through prayer in the world. This Lent, consider having a simplistic, minimalist prayer life that focuses less on what is around you and more on what is inside of you. This work and focus remind me of the first, second, and third stanzas of the poem by David Whyte, *Start Close In:*

> *Start close in,*
> *don't take the second step*
> *or the third,*
> *start with the first*
> *thing*
> *close in,*
> *the step*
> *you don't want to take.*
>
> *Start with*
> *the ground*
> *you know,*
> *the pale ground*
> *beneath your feet,*
> *your own*
> *way to begin*
> *the conversation.*
>
> *Start with your own*
> *question,*
> *give up on other*
> *people's questions,*
> *don't let them*
> *smother something*
> *simple.*[9]

---

[9] https://davidwhyte.com/.

The question I ask that you consider this Lent is, "Are you willing to give yourself permission to begin your prayer journey within?" When praying, focus and listen to what God is telling you and where God is directing you. This endeavor won't be easy because there are so many demands vying for our attention: other people, media, technology, internal conversations, work, traffic, the past, the present, and the future. To de-clutter and simplify takes work and commitment, especially in our prayer lives.

Jesus' words, "When you pray, pray like..." still resonate for us today as they compel us to look within before we project externally. Remember the words of David Whyte, "Don't let them smother something simple."

In my personal prayer life, I am trying to focus on the things within my control instead of those beyond my control. For instance, I can't control what happens thousands of miles across an ocean or a choice a close family member may make. I can, however, control my response to something that happens thousands of miles away from home or my response to a decision a close family member makes. It doesn't mean I don't have a global focus or global concern. I actually care deeply about God's world and creation but I have to ensure that my prayer life also focuses on what God is calling me to do with my life. When I begin at that point, it enables me to be a compassionate citizen of the world and to help and support others from the overflow of my life, and not out of the scarcity of my life.

My personal prayer life teaches me to focus more within and helps me to know how I need to respond and show up in the world. The only way I can accomplish this is by beginning my time in prayer by focusing on my relationship with God rather than on being heard publicly or developing prayer content that impresses me more than it impresses God. When I focus prayerfully internally first, I can live in the world and not be overwhelmed by what happens in the world.

The great theologian and mystic Howard Thurman illustrates this point in his book, *The Creative Encounter.* He says prayer is a crucial element to religious experience:

> *In the first place, prayer, in the sense in which I am using it, means the method by which the individual makes his [her] way to the temple of quiet within his [her] own spirit and the activity of his [her] spirit within its walls. Prayer is not only the participation in communication with God in the encounter of religious experience, but it is also the "readying" of the spirit for such communication.*[10]

This "readying" that Thurman speaks of is special and unique to the role of the church and how we, as

---

[10]  Howard Thurman. *The Creative Encounter* (Richmond, Indiana: Friends United Press, 1954), 34.

leaders, have a responsibility to help parishioners look within to discover and rediscover themselves and God. He goes on to say of this unique role of the church:

> *In such "readying," a quiet place is very important, if not altogether mandatory. In the noise of our times, such a place may be impossible to find. One of the great services that the Christian church can render to the community is to provide spells and spaces of quiet for the world-weary men and women whose needs are so desperate.*[11]

This instruction may not be easy to understand or follow in our current culture, where so many people seek fame and time in the spotlight. There is so much outward promotion and focus these days that it is easy to lose oneself or sell out to the lure of self-promotion and publicity.

Let me be clear. I am not saying you shouldn't build your brand or platform. There is, however, a line in the sand between allowing your brand/platform to *become* your purpose and passion for life and using your brand/platform to *highlight* your purpose and passion for life.

If Jesus were walking the Earth today, he might very well use social media and other tools for publicizing his ministry. One of the ways Jesus would have used

---

[11]   Ibid., 34-35.

social media would have been to fulfill the Great Commission. When Jesus gave the Great Commission to the disciples, he was not thinking local or regional; he was thinking global.

> *Go therefore and make disciples of all nations, baptizing them in the name of the Father and of the Son and of the Holy Spirit, and teaching them to obey everything that I have commanded you. And remember, I am with you always, to the end of the age.*
>
> **Matthew 28:19-20 (NRSV)**

Social media would have instantly taken the Great Commission to "all nations." Jesus' motivation and strategy for using social media would have been different. Perhaps Jesus would post daily prayer meditations. His desire would not be for people to follow him, but, instead, that they follow God. Conceivably, he might have the disciples buy commercial time on websites or during major sports games so that God's glory would be shared, not his own glory.

Jesus' instruction on prayer wasn't against public promotion of the Gospel but, rather, challenges us to evaluate our ego and motivation. In today's culture, we must constantly ask ourselves, Why are we doing what we are doing?

Jesus went on to say:

> *But thou, when thou prayest, enter into thy*
> *closet, and when thou has shut thy door, pray*
> *to thy Father which is in secret; and thy Father*
> *which seeth in secret shall reward thee openly.*

**Matthew 6:6 (KJV)**

Some people may only interpret what Jesus said in this passage literally and use it to guardrail their prayer lives, but this imagery is more symbolic than literal. Symbolically, this first-century example instructs us to be on guard and mindful of our prayer lives to ensure we aren't praying to the world but to God. Praying from our symbolic closets means praying from a place of authenticity lest our prayer lives become public spectacles or reruns of modern-day reality television shows.

Jesus' instructions on prayer direct us to practice self-reflection and awareness so that, when we engage the world through prayer, we can be fully present with God because we have been fully present with ourselves. To be fully present with self means spending quality time in prayer and allowing introspection to run the entire course in your mind and spirit.

This process is not about being alone or isolated in physical closets; it is about being comfortable alone with oneself in prayer. More than an image of a physical

30

place, it is an emotional and spiritual place that longs to receive us fully so that we can ultimately meet ourselves and God through prayer.

I encourage you to push aside the notion of a physical prayer room with four walls, floor, ceiling, and a door. Think of it as an internal space where God is wholly God; perhaps the prayers you offer will become more than words on a page and will become expressions of transformation in your life.

This transformation is what Lent is all about as we prepare for Easter. Through the process of reflection and introspection via prayer, we open our spirits to God's direction. Our transformation leads us to Easter, and when we arrive at Easter Sunday, we are changed and different. We celebrate the resurrection of Jesus, who overcame death and the grave, and we celebrate our own transformation as well. But, before we can fully celebrate Easter, we must work to transform ourselves through Lent and allow God's perfect work to refine and reshape us.

All of the spiritual disciplines you engage in during Lent are important, and I hope you practice each one in a fresh way. I also ask that you, during this Lenten season, attempt to see prayer through the eyes of Jesus. After all, he is teaching us how to pray today, just as he taught his disciples over two thousand years ago.

During Lent, the Lord's Prayer provides a spiritual path that allows believers to enter into introspection at their own resurrection, post-Lent, after having overcome the world like their Savior. For instance, during COVID, it was not uncommon for families to experience multiple losses and the all too familiar agonizing grief that comes with loss. Grief and loss are real, and the path to healing can be long and arduous. But even in these most difficult moments in life, like Christ, we discover a renewed hope and faith in knowing that life does not end at a loss but can begin again in new and profound ways.

As Christians, we know life did not end on Good Friday because if life ended on Good Friday, we would not be able to celebrate Easter. What will your post-resurrection self look like this Lent season? Who are you becoming? What is God doing in you? Where is God leading you?

Let's continue our journey together through Lent and arrive at the power and proclamation of Easter, knowing, like Christ, we too are alive and well and have overcome the world.

# Questions:

Are there times when you are more focused on the words of your prayer than the meaning of your prayer with God?

Do you think you can adopt a simple, simplistic, minimalist approach to prayer this Lent? What would it mean to de-clutter your prayer life?

How do you show up in the world through prayer?

Is the content of your prayer more about you than about your relationship with God? If so, how can you begin having conversations with God in prayer that focus on your relationship with God?

*Aide*
*Prayer*
*Protest*
*Announcement*

*Russel Morgan*
*George Floyd*
*Accountability*
*v Partner*

# CHAPTER TWO

# Hypocrisy (Hypocrites)

*Have mercy on me, God, according*
*to your faithful love!*

*Wipe away my wrongdoings according*
*to your great compassion!*

*Wash me completely clean of my guilt;*

*purify me from my sin!*

**Psalm 51:1-2 (CEB)**

**And whenever you pray, do not be like the hypocrites; for they love to stand and pray in the synagogues and at the street corners, so that they may be seen by others. Truly I tell you, they have received their reward.**

**Matthew 6:5 (NRSV)**

The words *hypocrisy* and *hypocrite* conjure powerful images and memories of times when someone misrepresented the truth through their actions and words. In this scripture, we speculate that Jesus may be referring to the Pharisees and Sadducees with whom he had a long-standing, tense relationship during his ministry. Mark recorded Jesus' teaching:

*Beware of the scribes, who like to walk around
in long robes, and to be greeted with respect
in the marketplaces, and to have the best
seats in the synagogues and places of honor at
banquets! They devour widows' houses and for
the sake of appearance say long prayers. They
will receive the greater condemnation.*

**Mark 12:38-40 (NRSV)**

In his book, *The Politics of Jesus*, biblical scholar Obery Hendricks, Jr., lists the following tension between Jesus and the Pharisees and the Sadducees: "…the priests' political quietism and their accommodation of Roman policies made them complicit in the Jews' subjugation."[12]

The Pharisees and Sadducees demonstrated religious piety and publicly righteousness. But privately, when it came to standing up to the Roman government, they did not fight for the rights of their fellow Jewish brothers and sisters.

The word *hypocrisy* describes a person who says one thing but does the exact opposite or a person who acts out a superficial part or role as opposed to being authentic. Ouch! *Hypocrisy* is not a new concept or behavior; it has existed since the beginning of time and is part of the human journey. After all, to live is to struggle with hypocrisy.

What makes this word and action so applicable is that even on the days when we are committed to doing

---

[12] Obery Hendricks, Jr. *The Politics of Jesus* (New York: Doubleday. New York, 2006), 61.

everything the absolute right way to honor our word and commitments, we fall short and, in essence, are hypocrites. Scripture reminds us:

**_All have sinned and fall short of the glory of God._**
**Romans 3:23 (NRSV)**

The hypocrites Jesus referred to in Matthew wrestled with maintaining alignment of their public and private behavior and believed that allowing people to see them pray aloud in public settings would elevate them to something they weren't privately. Of course, we can only speculate about the contrast between their public and private lives. Still, for the Pharisees and the Sadducees, there was clearly more emphasis on being publicly honored and righteous than privately fulfilling God's will. This problematic alignment of our public and private selves summarizes the historical tension of the human condition with hypocrisy.

As a clergyperson, I am well aware of the expectations and pressure some people place on particular vocations – especially those in ministry – to constantly live a life of personal and public alignment.

This battle to align the public and private self is real, and if we aren't careful, we can become hypocrites in our words and deeds, acting one way publicly and living the opposite privately.

For Jesus, it was all about motivation and intent. I don't believe Jesus used this warning about hypocrites to mandate perfection but, rather, to examine one's motivation and intent. The hypocrites Jesus spoke of in Matthew 6:5 were motivated by public applause and recognition instead of personal piety and a relationship with God built on humility and genuine concern for others.

As a pastor, I have prayed thousands of times publicly: during worship, before church meetings, at public events, and so on. Admittedly, there were times when I led these public prayers, and my heart and intent weren't in the right place.

For example, suppose I wanted to impress people with my "God-talk" and my ability to connect words and phrases. In that case, I might pray longer than was necessary and forget that my role was to be part of the worship experience, not the main attraction.

Looking back on some of those prayers, I thank God for grace because even when my motivation and intent weren't centered around God, grace and the Holy Spirit were still at work, and the people were blessed. Have you ever been guilty of trying to impress people with your impressive "God-talk," and instead of fully being present in the room or conversation, you were more concerned about impressing the audience? If your answer is yes, you are not alone because we have all been there and the hope is that we don't have to stay in that place and be willing to focus more on

God than on trying to impress people.

Now that I have lived a little longer and had more opportunities to pray with people publicly and privately, I can earnestly say my prayer life has shifted from being less about me and more about God. I am less concerned about what people think and more concerned about what people need.

Making this shift reminds me of some of the preachers I grew up knowing as mentors who would pray a prayer of consecration before their sermon. The prayer went a little like this, "God, hide me behind the cross of Christ so that the people see you and not me." I believe those preachers were authentically attempting to align themselves with God so as not to practice hypocrisy, and it was vital for them to ask God for help. One of my favorite public and private prayers of alignment comes from scripture:

> *Let the words of my mouth and*
> *the meditation of my heart*
> *be acceptable to you,*
> *O Lord, my rock and my redeemer.*

**Psalm 19:14 (NRSV)**

This scripture-based prayer is the one I frequently say before I preach or speak to a public audience, but even more so, it is part of my daily personal prayer life. I wish I could write that I am always a model example of my words and the meditations of my heart are always acceptable to God, but most days, they aren't. Thankfully, God loves me anyway, and that knowledge inspires me to rejoice and try each day to live more faithfully to God's will.

Trust me, talking about how not to be a hypocrite is easier said than done because hypocrisy has a stronghold on every area where we live and exist, in our culture, how we treat others, and how we make decisions. As a citizen of the United States, I realize I have certain privileges and benefits that people in other countries do not have. This realization became increasingly evident with the release of the COVID-19 vaccine. As parts of the world were struggling to get their vaccination rates simply into the double digits, the United States was discarding unused vaccines and stockpiling them at the same time.

In September 2021, NBC News reported startling facts regarding vaccine waste:

> *Pharmacies and state governments in the United States have thrown away at least 15.1 million doses of COVID-19 vaccines since March 1, according to government data obtained by NBC News – a far larger number than previously known and still probably an undercount.*[13]

---

[13] Joshua Eaton and Joe Murphy. (2021, September 1). 15 million Covid vaccine doses thrown away in the U.S. since March, new data shows. NBC News. https://www.nbcnews.com/news/us-news/america-has-wasted-least-15-million-covid-vaccine-doses-march-n1278211.

The same article quoted Sharifah Sekalala, an associate professor of global health law at England's University of Warwick, saying, "A lot of the global south is unvaccinated. The African continent is still below 10 percent, and that's just a huge inequality, and it's really problematic."[14] Professor Sekalala was right, and although there are some valid reasons for discarding vaccine doses, the sad truth is that only a few countries in the world possess the most wealth, healthcare resources and technology, and can offer their citizens more help quickly.

I am not trying to debate about what the countries with resources should or should not do. I am, however, asking you to think critically as a Christian. Do you think Jesus would be pleased with our nation expressing love to its own people while, at the same time, holding on to vital health resources that could help eradicate a pandemic around the world? We must not forget that Jesus' model prayer wasn't local or regional; it was global.

If we say we are Christian and love all people, we must advocate for all people in all places. Jesus' words to the nations about caring for the least of these still ring in our ears today:

---

14    Ibid.

*Then the righteous will answer him, "Lord,
when was it that we saw you hungry and gave
you food, or thirsty and gave you something
to drink? And when was it that we saw you a
stranger and welcomed you, or naked and gave
you clothing? And when was it that we saw
you sick or in prison and visited you?" And the
king will answer them, "Truly I tell you, just
as you did it to one of the least of these who are
members of my family, you did it to me.*

**Matthew 25:37-40 (NRSV)**

Still today, with a global community suffering from war, disease, famine, and inequality, we too, like the righteous people in Jesus' time on Earth, are guilty of being hypocrites as we have focused more on ourselves than God's people and God's world.

Jesus encourages us to go into our closets and evaluate ourselves so that when we pray, we aren't actors pretending to love all people; we are fully committed, through our words and deeds, to be the hands and feet of Christ. This type of prayer and prayer readiness is crucial because some people may never read the Bible, walk into a church, or attend a small virtual group, but they will meet you, and you may be the only Jesus they see.

You may be thinking this is all too overwhelming. You may feel like Jesus' disciples who turned away and said, "This teaching is difficult; who can accept it?"

(John 6:60 NRSV). Like these disciples, during Lent, you may feel the call to action Jesus proclaims in the Lord's Prayer is too difficult, but hang in there and trust that God's grace is *for* you and *with* you. When you mess up, give yourself a break. Don't be too hard on yourself, and remember, in the latter verses of the Lord's Prayer, Jesus addresses our mistakes and temptations and covers them with God's grace and forgiveness. Breathe and thank God for Jesus.

## Questions:

This Lent, can you identify an example in your own life where you have been a hypocrite? If so, did you realize it at the time or upon later reflection? Can you think of a recent time when your public and private actions did not align?

Have you ever struggled with aligning your public and private self? If so, was there something that helped you achieve alignment?

Is it possible to be a Christian and be connected to organizations, institutions, or a government that doesn't always represent your faith? If so, how do you reconcile it?

Do you find it easy to point out the hypocrisy of others but difficult to see the hypocrisy in your own actions?

# CHAPTER THREE

# An Inclusive God and Holy God

> *God is spirit, and it is necessary*
> *to worship God in spirit and truth.*
>
> **John 4:24 (CEB)**

*Our Father in Heaven, hallowed be your name.*

**Matthew 6:9 (NRSV)**

In this chapter, I want to focus on the concept of space. I'm not talking about the type of space we refer to when discussing NASA or the race for ordinary citizens to orbit the Earth's atmosphere in a space shuttle. The concept of space I am talking about is the space of inclusion. This type of space gives people permission to show up and fully be themselves in mind, body, and spirit. In this space, children can dream big dreams without fear of failure or ridicule. In this space, all people are treated fairly, regardless of color or creed. In this inclusive space, every one counts and matters to God and each other.

Because inclusion is a big priority in our church, Impact Church in East Point, Georgia, we intentionally adopted the current vision statement:

*An inclusive gathering of people committed to holistic salvation and doing Christ's work in the world.* [15]

Across the globe, many cultures, governments, organizations, and systems recognize the importance of inclusion, and people seek to be more equitable in their treatment of others. I don't have a utopian view of where the world stands with equality, but I believe we are making strides in the right direction and must continue to do so. I also think the Lord's Prayer offers us an opportunity to address inclusion in a significant, meaningful way, especially if we use inclusive language when referring to God.

I am grateful for the awareness and work to help all people – especially transgender people – feel more welcome through our sensitivity to pronouns.

Living through the pandemic and attending more Zoom meetings than you can count, you probably have a Ph.D. in Zoom Meetings 101. During some Zoom meetings, participants list their names and the pronouns they use to identify themselves, i.e., she/her, he/him, they/them, and so on.

The LGBTQ advocacy group GLSEN published a paper entitled, *Pronouns: A Resource.* The writing helps explain why we often see pronouns listed under names on a Zoom call or name tag:

---

[15]  https://www.impactdcd.org.

*This gives everyone in the room the opportunity to self identify instead of assuming someone's identity or which pronouns they use. Including pronouns is a first step toward respecting people's identity and creating a more welcoming space for people of all genders.*[16]

Listing one's pronouns below or beside their name gives the person they are talking to a direct link to the gender they identify with, so no assumptions are made related to gender identification. I am grateful for this work and effort to make space for all people, especially those in our society who are the most marginalized and oppressed. We need to make space for inclusion.

In our current culture, we are making strides to create more space for inclusion and what it means to see people as they are and to embrace and accept them fully. We have seen this with religion, race, politics, culture, sexual orientation, gender, and geography. But, even with these great strides toward inclusion, some of us have not entirely made this shift and transition theologically in the way we see, view, and name God.

Historically and up to recent decades, we have assigned male pronouns to God, saying "He," "Him," and "His" when referring to our Creator. But this begs the question: Is God a man? The exclusive, noninclusive, limited space answer is yes. The infinite

---

[16] https://www.glsen.org/activity/pronouns-guide-glsen.

and inclusive answer is, "No, God is God."

During Moses' call at the burning bush in the Old Testament, Moses asked God who God was, and God said, "I AM WHO I AM" (Exodus 3:14 NRSV). In the New Testament, in John's Gospel, God is neither male nor female, but Jesus referred to God as a "spirit." This part of the Lord's Prayer reinforces an image of God as father/male, but I hope this Lenten season and beyond you will be able to see God as God and know that God's name-gender, essence, and being is God.

I know this may be a big ask and stretch, but journey with me and give the God of creation the space to be more than a father or a mother. Give God room in your theology to be God, "I Am."

So how do we address the fact that Jesus began the Lord's Prayer with "Our Father?" To unpack this significant salutation, I first start not – in Matthew's Gospel – but in John's Gospel with a woman at a well having a conversation with Jesus. When pressed with the concern over where and when to worship God, Jesus said:

> **God is spirit, and it is necessary to worship God in spirit and truth.**
>
> **John 4:24 (CEB)**

It is important to note that although Jesus referred to God as "Father" at the beginning of the Lord's Prayer in Matthew, in John's Gospel, he states that God is a spirit that has no gender or form. This passage releases God from gender-pronoun boundaries and the male images of God we hold in our minds. For centuries, artists have helped reinforce these images of a male God, as Michelangelo did in his famous painting in the Sistine Chapel. So, what do we do with these words and images of God as father, male, and man that are seared into our psyche? Let's take a moment to think through the following questions.

## Who is God?

When we think about who God is, it is easy to assign God a gender that is typically male and describe God as "Father," "He," or "Him." The Hebrews used a different name for God in the Old Testament: *Yahweh*. David Wheeler-Reed wrote:

> *In fact, the personal name of God, YAHWEH, as revealed to Moses in Exodus 3, is a remarkable combination of both female and male grammatical endings. The first part of God's name in Hebrew, "Yah," is feminine, and the last part, "weh," is masculine.* [17]

In Exodus Chapter 3, in verse 14, God declares God's

---

[17] David Wheeler-Reed. (2018, August 1). What the early church thought about God's gender. *The Conversation.* https://theconversation.com/what-the-early-church-thought-about-gods-gender-100077.

name as "I Am Who I Am," which is translated:

*I will be who I will be.*

Exodus 3:14 (CEB)

The short answer to the question, "Who is God?" is that God is God, or YAHWEH, or I Am. As humans, we naturally need and desire to attribute human characteristics to God so that we might better identify with, and relate to, the God we cannot see. In our need to connect to God, we often assign a gender label to God, but the truth is, any gender label you give God is inaccurate. This Lenten season, consider allowing yourself to see and know God as God, YAHWEH, or I Am.

## What is God?

Jesus clearly said that God is a spirit, and a spirit is not a human or in human form. In our need to describe God from an anthropological point of view to identify with God, we often box God into the image and symbols that attempt to describe what God is to other people or explain God in our "God-talk" through sermons, literature, prayers, worship, and general conversation. By doing this, we sometimes communicate that God is a man or a person, but the "what" of God is spirit, not human. To name God by any other label doesn't actually limit God but speaks more to how we see and relate to God. We, consciously or unconsciously, try to identify with God by making God a person, but God is not a person.

## Where is God?

When we reflect on the location of God, we have typically learned that God is in Heaven. Although this is accurate, it is not the complete story because God is omnipresent: God is at all places at all times. To say God is only in Heaven is similar to characterizing God solely as a male. Unlike God, we can only be in one place at one time, and this is why we say, "God is God, and we are not."

God is everywhere, in all places at the same time. I know this is hard to fathom, but that is one reason God is God and not human or in human form. It is mind-blowing to know that God is in Heaven and present in all of the continents in the world, and at the same time, God is even present beyond the world itself. Being omnipresent is pretty cool. It sounds like a superpower one possesses in a modern-day action film that keeps you tied to the screen. You are amazed when you see the character leap from the rooftops of skyscrapers and suddenly appear in another location on the opposite side of the globe.

As cool as this may be, God still has the upper hand because God doesn't have to travel to appear in another location around the world. God is already there. When I realize this, my prayer life evolved from sending God to the hospital, prison, or someone's home to saying, "God, I acknowledge that you are already in all places at the same time, and I thank you for already being there."

When we consider who, what, and where God is, it makes the case that God is a spirit, and any human attachment to God limits our understanding of God. Because we are human, though, it helps us identify with God by adding human attributes to God. When I was in seminary, our professors insisted we use inclusive language when referring to God, which meant deleting pronouns when we referenced God. The truth is, our grade depended on it.

I realize this is a controversial concept for many people, especially those who have grown up in churches that never addressed inclusive language and always used the default images of God as a man. It took time for me to get it – and a few marks on my papers – but I finally got it academically, spiritually, and theologically. As I learned more about inclusive language and how it gives liberty to see God in more than the image of a man, I also learned that some people might embrace the image of God as a female and refer to God as a mother or woman.

The good news is that we know there is a God, and whatever pronoun we attach to God is about our personal relationship with God, not what the world says we should say or how we should view God. There is great liberty in viewing and describing God if we choose to make space and embrace inclusive language and inclusive theology. Like the woman at the well in John's Gospel, we remain limited in our view of God until someone helps us see that God is bigger and greater than any description or label we place on God.

I admit this understanding of God was not easy for me to grasp when I was first introduced to it. Still, over time and through my growth in my personal relationship with God, I have let go of the restrictions I placed on God. I now embrace inclusive space for the omnipresent (all-present) and omniscient (all-knowing) God, even when I can never wholly describe or understand God.

Maybe this is an opportunity for you to begin the Lord's Prayer differently, refer to God as God, or choose to assign God a pronoun or description that speaks to your relationship. Here are a few versions to consider at the beginning of the Lord's Prayer:

- Our Mother in Heaven

- Our Friend in Heaven

- Our Creator in Heaven

- Our God in Heaven

- Our Savior in Heaven

At first, these examples may seem uncomfortable for you to read or hear, but give them a try and see how they resonate in your spirit. You never know; you may discover your past descriptions of God no longer fit your current personal relationship with God.

After Jesus began the prayer with "Our Father," he then said, "hallowed be your name" (Matthew 6:9 NRSV). *Hallowed* means that God is holy, set apart, high, and uplifted. To be holy is to be honored and set apart. Wherever God is present, that very place is sacred.

In Exodus, during God's "I Am" conversation with Moses, God said, "Don't come any closer! Take off your sandals, because you are standing on holy ground" (Exodus 3:5 NRSV). The ground where Moses was standing was holy because God was there.

In another instance, when Moses asked to see God's face, God replied to Moses, "You can't see my face because no one can see me and live." The LORD said:

> *Here is a place near me where you will stand beside the rock. As my glorious presence passes by, I'll set you in a gap in the rock, and I'll cover you with my hand until I've passed by. Then I'll take away my hand, and you will see my back, but my face won't be visible.*
>
> **Exodus 33:20-23 (CEB)**

This whole notion of God being holy and set apart is demonstrated in Exodus as Moses is in direct relationship and conversation with God. Yet, because God's name and presence are holy, Moses can't fully see God.

Isaiah, too, speaks of God's name as holy in the unforgettable scene where he sees God in the midst of a heavenly host and one of the angels announces:

> *Holy, holy, holy is the Lord of hosts;*
> *the whole Earth is full of his glory.*
>
> **Isaiah 6:3 (NRSV)**

Earlier in the chapter, I encouraged you to rethink the masculine pronouns when referring to God and see God for God, but there are other names given to God that are holy and set apart. Here are a few:

**Jehovah Jireh:** *The LORD our provider* **(Genesis 22:14)**

**Jehovah Rapha:** *The LORD our Healer* **(Exodus 15:26)**

**Jehovah Nissi:** *The LORD our Banner* **(Exodus 17:15)**

**Jehovah Shalom:** *The LORD our Peace* **(Judges 6:24)**

**Jehovah Raah:** *The LORD our Shepherd* **(Psalms 23:1)**

**Jehovah Tsidkenu:** *The LORD our Righteousness*
**(Jeremiah 23:6)**

**Jehovah Shammah:** *The LORD is Here* **(Ezekiel 48:35)**[18]

---

[18]  Danielle Bernock. (2020, June 8). What Are All the Names of God Found in the Bible? *Christianity.com.* https://www.christianity.com/wiki/god/what-are-all-the-names-of-god.html.

Each of these names of God represents God's specific characteristics and what it means for God's name to be holy and set apart.

The name God sets God apart from any other being or deity because God's name is holy, and because God's name is holy, whenever we pray, we should be reminded that we are in the presence of God, the presence of holiness. As God told Moses to take off his shoes because he was standing on holy ground, God is telling us to be mindful because we are praying to a holy God, you are praying and standing on holy ground.

Whatever and whenever you pray this Lent, know you have an audience with God and God alone. I say this not as a note of caution about the formality or tradition of prayer but rather to emphasize your awareness of God's presence and holiness whenever and wherever you pray. Being mindful of God's presence releases us from the traditional restraints of prayer and frees us to pray to God wherever we may happen to be because God is everywhere. Since God is everywhere, we are always in the presence of God's holiness. Even now, you are standing on holy ground in the presence of a holy God.

# Questions:

Do you believe God is a woman, man, or spirit? Explain.

How might you describe God to a nonbeliever?

What pronouns do you use to describe God? Are you open to using inclusive language when you describe God?

When you pray, are you conscious of God's holiness?

How does God's name being holy impact the way you see the world?

# CHAPTER FOUR

# Here and Now! Kingdom Come

*"We believe in you, O God, for you have made
the suffering of humanity your suffering.*

*You have come to establish a kingdom
of the poor and humble.*

*Today we sing to you, because you are alive,
you have saved us, you have made us free. Amen[19]*

***Your kingdom come. Your will be done, on earth
as it is in heaven.***

**Matthew 6:10 (NRSV)**

When we look at the world today, it isn't always easy
to see consistent reminders of God's Kingdom. Families
have been devastated by the COVID-19 pandemic and
continue to adjust to a world that will never be the same.
The global economy has taken a significant hit, and the
supply chain has been substantially impacted. Major
cities in the United States are dealing with a rise in
violent crimes and homicides.

One startling news report shared the following FBI

---

[19] *United Methodist Book of Worship* #511, United Methodist Publishing House, 1992.

statistics: "…a nearly 30% increase in murders in 2020, the largest single-year jump since the bureau began recording crime statistics six decades ago. The surge in killings drove an overall 5% increase in violent crime last year, according to the FBI's Uniform Crime Report."[20]

> *In addition, poverty and hunger continue to devastate Ethiopia: "Famine has afflicted at least 350,000 people in northern Ethiopia's conflict-ravaged Tigray region, a starvation calamity bigger at the moment than anywhere else in the world."*[21]

These are just a few global statistics on the state of our world, but they are more than enough to make one question the presence of God's Kingdom on Earth. Even as the world seems to be getting closer to a post-COVID-19 reality, we are still living with the trauma of the experience and living through a pandemic. Years from now, when families look back over their ancestry, because of the pandemic, some families will literally see several people who died in a single year from COVID-19. To have one family member die from COVID-19 can be devastating, and to have several die in one year is devastating and life-altering, so much so that it may take

---

[20] Kevin Johnson. (2021, September 27). FBI: Record surge in 2020 murders; nearly 30% increase drives spike in violent crime. *USA Today.* https://www.usatoday.com/story/news/politics/2021/09/27/fbi-reports-2020-murder-surge-biggest-single-year-jump/5886792001/.

[21] Rick Gladstone. (2021, June 10). Famine Hits 350,000 in Ethiopia, Worst-Hit Country in a Decade. *The New York Times.* https://www.nytimes.com/2021/06/10/world/africa/ethiopia-famine-tigray.html

some families and individuals years to adjust to the new normal, rediscover joy and live life fully. Whether you are reading crime reports, health care reports, or emotional well-being reports, all is not well in our world, and because of that, it causes us to wonder if God's Kingdom can be a reality right now or is it what we hope to see one day?

Sadly, we also see the pain and hurt many children are experiencing in the world. Later in Matthew's Gospel, Jesus acknowledged children and their ownership in the Kingdom of Heaven:

> *Allow the children to come to me," Jesus said. "Don't forbid them, because the Kingdom of Heaven belongs to people like these children.*
> **Matthew 19:14 (CEB)**

Maybe I am confused, but when I see the global pain and despair many children are in, I struggle to see God's Kingdom on Earth, and I genuinely don't see where the children have ownership of the kingdom. The words "Your kingdom come" seem more of an aspiration than reality because, even when Jesus walked the earth, it was not a perfect reflection of God's Kingdom.

Children live in poverty and hunger around the world. In the community where I serve as pastor, the "Child Well-Being Score" is only 34.7. That translates to lower birth rates, fewer students being proficient or above third-grade reading standards and eighth-grade math standards and fewer youth graduating from high school.[22] These statistics inspired our local church to focus on three key areas to change the statistics to praise reports of health and vitality. The three key areas are:

- Healthy Living
- Educational Success
- Workforce Readiness.

The goal of Healthy Living is:

> *Enabling and empowering individuals, seniors, and families to pursue healthy living across four holistic health pillars: mental/emotional, physical, social, and spiritual.*

One of the goals of Educational Success is to have a:

> *...positive impact on reading and math achievement.*

The main goal of Workforce Readiness is to:

> *Provide exposure to careers, access to jobs, and overall readiness to residents with career-building opportunities, with a focus on entrepreneurship and emerging industries.*[23]

I know these goals and dreams may seem idealistic.

---

[22] Unitedwayatlanta.org.

[23] Impact Church 2021.

Still, to our church and our community, they aren't because they represent God's Kingdom on Earth and raising our children to have the best opportunities for success available. I pray for the day when God's Kingdom is evident in all children's lives, regardless of where they are born in the world.

The prayer Jesus prayed is not only a request that God's Kingdom come and be an actuality on Earth but that we would do all we can to make God's Kingdom visible on Earth. As Christ's disciples, we are called to create a world where we are not only inspired by the prophet Isaiah's words, we are convicted to fulfill the prophecy through our actions:

> *The spirit of the Lord God is upon me,*
> *because the Lord has anointed me;*
> *he has sent me to bring good news to the*
> *oppressed, to bind up the brokenhearted,*
> *to proclaim liberty to the captives,*
> *and release to the prisoners;*
> *to proclaim the year of the Lord's favor,*
> *and the day of vengeance of our God;*
> *to comfort all who mourn;*
> *to provide for those who mourn in Zion –*
> *to give them a garland instead of ashes,*
> *the oil of gladness instead of mourning,*
> *the mantle of praise instead of a faint spirit.*
>
> **Isaiah 61:1-3 (NRSV)**

We will know when God's Kingdom is on Earth

63

and when we are participating in the kingdom when, in addition to praying the Lord's Prayer, we live out the words of Isaiah, and as God's Spirit leads us, we ensure all of God's children are free from any hindrance or obstruction preventing them from being all that they can be.

In some cases, we have settled and become satisfied with our own kingdoms, forsaking God's Kingdom. There is a difference. Our kingdoms are built around ego and self, which create walls of class and distinction. These kingdoms don't represent hope, liberation, love, and joy; they represent exclusion and judgment.

When we focus on our kingdoms and not God's Kingdom, we live life selfishly and miss out on rich and abundant relationships with other people who help us grow and develop in our faith and understanding of the world. Our kingdoms are small, limited, self-centered, and unable to create the generative resources the world needs to exist and thrive.

However, God's Kingdom is expansive, global, and welcomes all people from all walks of life and cultures. In God's Kingdom, the gates and walls are torn down, and people can freely come and go, receiving God's grace, favor, and love. The question to ponder today is, Whose kingdom are you asking to come? Is it your kingdom or God's Kingdom?

What would God's Kingdom look like today? There is no way to answer this question entirely, but a few signs of the kingdom would be these:

- All children have access to the best private or public schools and receive the best education regardless of their zip code

- Health care would be provided for those without means, and the level of care would be the same for everyone

- No person would be left behind in the economy

- There would be no barriers among people

- Conversations would be kinder

- Forgiveness would be extended

- Grace would be the baseline of all relationships and interactions

When we surrender our personal kingdoms and embrace God's Kingdom, we help God's Kingdom become real on Earth. We all have a responsibility to help "thy Kingdom come" on Earth in our own contextual ways.

Over the years, I have met people who help to bring God's Kingdom to Earth in their own way. One is Terence Lester, a friend who engages in a mobile homeless ministry in Metro Atlanta called *Love Beyond Walls.*

On his website, *lovebeyondwalls.org,* Terence issued an open letter of apology to the homeless community. One of the lines reads:

*Today, I want to apologize to you if you're
experiencing homelessness and have been judged,
overlooked, walked by, and abused by the words
of people who have never walked in your shoes.* [24]

Terence has been on the front lines of helping the
unhoused and making God's Kingdom a reality on
Earth. I thank God for the work of Love Beyond Walls
and other similar organizations serving as the hands
and feet of Christ.

I have another friend, Milton Little, Jr., who leads
one of the largest United Ways in the United States,
United Way of Greater Atlanta. Milton serves as the
president and CEO, and their four investment areas are
Strong Leaders, College and Career Ready, Economic
Stability, and Brighter Future. The website lists the
following inspiration about helping children:

*Every child whose life we change will go on to
change the lives of countless other children,
families, and communities. And when we work
together – pooling our resources, time, and
energy – our community impact grows exponen-
tially to create an equitable future for all. Let's
do MORE, together."* [25]

These words are eternal, and more than a series
of phrases put together. They are a call to action for
anyone willing to take seriously being change agents in

---

[24] https://www.lovebeyondwalls.org/open-apology-to-people-experiencing-homelessness-during-covid-19/. Accessed November 1, 2021.

[25] https://www.unitedwayatlanta.org/child-well-being-map.

the world and surrendering their lives for the sake of making someone else's life better.

I have another friend that I equally admire who anonymously pays it forward through service and support of others through financial generosity. When the pandemic started in 2020, she reached out and donated $20,000 to help feed families. At the beginning of the pandemic, while most people were finding creative ways to store away funds, she was giving away funds to help others.

I admire each of these friends and so many others I know personally, or through stories of their lives, who strive every day to make God's Kingdom a reality on Earth their own way. They indeed are the hands and feet of Christ, a part of the solution. I honor them, and I thank God for them.

Notice this chapter title includes the words "Here and Now!" expressing the dire need and yearning for God's Kingdom not to be prolonged or delayed any longer but to be present "Here and Now!" The anxiety and fear we face day-to-day create this urgent longing in our lives. Have you ever woken up in the morning and thought, What will happen today? Do you feel that something negative or tragic might happen in your life, in the life of someone you knew, or somewhere around the world?

After serving as a pastor, there are days, weeks, and months when I wonder, *What will happen next?* When I raise this question, I am not expecting something good to happen. I know this may sound like doom and gloom, but when you work in a profession where you receive the very best and the worst news in the course of a day, you may develop a thought pattern that raises the question, *What will happen next?*

If I am not careful, I can get trapped in a negative narrative and only see the world from a doom-and-gloom perspective instead of a hopeful, grateful place. This negative thought process can last a lifetime. We can see it in the lives of people we love who seem to be trapped in this never-ending narrative of tragedy and trauma because they have lost hope, no longer believe the world can change, or that people are inherently good.

Even in Jesus' earthly ministry, some had lost hope in the fulfillment of the Old Testament prophets forecasting a future savior and wondered if the words of Isaiah would really come true:

> *For a child has been born for us, a son given to us; authority rests upon his shoulders; and he is named Wonderful Counselor, Mighty God, Everlasting Father, Prince of Peace.*
>
> **Isaiah 9:6 (NRSV)**

When will the child be born? When will the government be upon his shoulders? When will my world change for the better? Not only did they ask these questions two thousand years ago, but we still ask these same questions today.

There is a yearning sense of urgency when we ask

for God's Kingdom to come here on Earth. As you journey through Lent and experience grace and forgiveness, are there places in your church, community, and family where God's Kingdom seems far away and distant, and you need God's Kingdom here and now? When you see events happening on the other side of the globe that are painful, do you desire God's Kingdom here and now? When you see and experience close and personal events, do you wish for God's Kingdom here and now?

We should first pray daily for God's Kingdom to come on Earth here and now and then we need to do everything we can to embody God's Kingdom here and now. This part of the Lord's Prayer should be part of our daily prayer lives – the moment we pray for God's Kingdom to become a reality on Earth here and now, *and* to do everything we can to embody God's Kingdom here and now. God's Kingdom becomes real on Earth when we surrender our personal kingdoms and represent God's Kingdom.

Surrendering our personal kingdoms is a soul-wrenching challenge because it means giving up some of our limited human hopes and dreams and adopting God's will for a life greater than anything we can ever imagine. Letting go of our personal kingdoms means being able to surrender everything like Jesus did in the Garden of Gethsemane. Even Jesus thought of places he would rather be than dying on the cross. Instead, he surrendered to God's will and endured the excruciating, agonizing pain of the cross – for us.

69

In his book *The Politics of Jesus*, Obery Hendricks, Jr., describes crucifixion:

> *Similar to the phenomenon of "lynchings" in the modern era, public crucifixions were intended to strike terror in the hearts of those who were lorded over...Although terrible enough, the several hours Jesus hung on the cross were atypically short. Most victims of crucifixion took much longer to die. Some hung immobilized for days before breathing their last.[26]*

Before and after the death of Jesus, there have been countless persons who have died for the cause of freedom and justice, hoping to help bring God's Kingdom to Earth, even until their last breath. Scripture in Hebrews reminds us of these pioneers of our faith:

> *Others suffered mocking and flogging, and even chains and imprisonment. They were stoned to death, they were sawn in two, they were killed by the sword; they went about in skins of sheep and goats, destitute, persecuted, tormented – of whom the world was not worthy. They wandered in deserts and mountains, and in caves and holes in the ground. Yet all these, though they were commended for their faith, did not receive what was promised, since God had provided something better so that they would not, apart from us, be made perfect.*

> **Hebrews 11:36-40 (NRSV)**

---

[26] Obery Hendricks, Jr. *The Politics of Jesus.* (New York: Doubleday, 2006), 51.

70

Although Jesus made the greatest, ultimate sacrifice for God's Kingdom to become real on Earth, so many others sacrificed their lives, too. The Book of Hebrews names these persons and beautifully describes their stories, and today, we continue to lift the names of sheroes and heroes who took that last breath on this side of glory while looking to Heaven and praying, "Your kingdom come."

Because of these sacrifices, we must do all we can do each day to bring about love, peace, and justice for all people in hopes that, one day, we can genuinely say that Heaven and Earth are identical.

How might we accomplish this? A great place to start is with humility and generosity. Humility is recognizing that we are not perfect and the world we live in is not perfect. Because of this fact, we cannot be judges or juries of anyone. In his book *Positive Intelligence*, Shirzad Chamine reveals the concept of "Saboteurs," which he describes as our internal enemies. He makes the point that the worst saboteur we have is the judge:

> *The Judge is the master Saboteur, the one everyone suffers from. It compels you to constantly find faults with yourself, others, and your conditions and circumstances.*[27]

Sound familiar? For many of us, judging is quite

---

[27] Shirzad Chamine. *Positive Intelligence* (Austin, Texas: Greenleaf Book Group Press, 2016), 16-17.

natural because we are born into environments that teach us to judge other people. Maybe a commercial on television showed a bias towards another culture, or perhaps you overheard adults judging each other when you were a child. The fact about judging is it can be a hard habit to break and a difficult pattern to undo. In God's Kingdom, there is no space for judgment.

I exercise at a national fitness chain, and when I walk through the entrance, I am greeted with the words in bold print on the wall, "Judgment Free Zone." These impactful words boldly announce to customers that they are accepted where they are and that everyone in the fitness center is on a personal journey towards living a healthier life. If a national fitness chain can practice an ethic of acceptance without judgment, the church of Jesus Christ and Christians should be able to do this as well.

Another way to embody God's Kingdom on Earth is through generosity. When we talk or write about generosity, it is easy to shift quickly to thoughts of money, but generosity is about much more than money. My faith tradition speaks about generosity in three forms: time, talents, and treasure. The money part (treasure) is last because there are so many forms of generosity that have nothing to do with money. I don't write this to limit the value of money, but rather to remind us that money isn't everything. We can miss vital opportunities to embody God's Kingdom on Earth if we only wait to do that through currency.

There have been innumerable examples and witnesses of people generously sharing their time and talents with brothers and sisters in need during the pandemic. For example, one news report highlights a person who makes meals in his home and delivers them to those in need. By doing this, he uses his talents to offer generosity. There are countless stories about people who have shared their time virtually during the pandemic to stay in touch with others and remind them of God's grace and God's love.

The lesson of generosity is that in addition to your treasure, God also wants your time and talents. When we share our time, talents, and treasure with the world, we come closer to God's Kingdom, a kingdom where humility and generosity reign supreme and selfishness and greed are sidelined.

We have a lot of work to do if we wish to partner with God and help God's Kingdom come here and now. Although the work is not easy, it is possible if we remember to practice humility and generosity with our fellow brothers and sisters.

# Questions:

When you pray the Lord's Prayer, whose kingdom are you asking to come: your kingdom or God's Kingdom?

What do personal kingdoms look like in your experience?

What would God's Kingdom look like here on Earth?

Why is it urgent for God's Kingdom to be evident on Earth?

What can you do in your context to make God's Kingdom on Earth a reality?

As you focus on Lent and go through the journey of grace and forgiveness, are there places in your church, community, and family where God's Kingdom seems far away and distant, and like Jesus, you need God's Kingdom here and now?

Do you see signs of God's Kingdom on Earth here and now? What are those signs?

# CHAPTER FIVE

# **Your Will**

> *"[God], if it's your will, take this cup of suffering away from me. However, not my will but your will must be done.*
>
> **Luke 22:42 (CEB)**

*Your will be done, on earth as it is in heaven.*
**Matthew 6:10 (NRSV)**

One of the most consistent questions people ask about God is, "How do I know if it is God's will?" In people's longing and desire to live according to God's plan, they battle with fully understanding what God would have them do.

A basic, legal understanding of a will is:

*A legal document that sets forth your wishes regarding the distribution of your property and the care of any minor children.*[28]

The key phrase is "sets forth your wishes." We use

---

[28] Lisa Smith. (2021, April 25). What Is a Will and Why Do I Need One Now? *Investopedia.* https://www.investopedia.com/articles/pf/08/what-is-a-will.asp.

legal wills to help direct those who have care over our property and resources after we die so that they will know our wishes and desires for our loved ones. God's will is similar in that it is God's "set of wishes" to help direct and guide our life on a specific path and plan.

Whenever someone asks, "How do you know if it is God's will," I encourage them to get to know God. Getting to know God is more than knowing God casually by going to church once or twice a year or praying a rote prayer on holidays from a book or Christian resource. Although these spiritual exercises are good – and I am not discouraging them – they don't necessarily mean you know God personally. When a person writes a will, they usually enlist someone they know to be the executor because they feel that person will be aware of and honor their wishes because they have a relationship.

Consider the following example of knowing someone's wishes. Imagine you and a close friend who has a severe food allergy are at a restaurant looking forward to eating a wonderful meal. The two of you order food, and before the food arrives, your friend excuses herself from the table. While she is away, the waiter delivers your meals, and you quickly notice the chef prepared your friend's meal with an ingredient to which she is allergic. You politely tell the waiter and ask that the dish be removed as soon as possible.

What might you see that is missing in this example?

If your response to the question was, "You didn't talk to your friend before you sent their meal back," you are correct. Why? Because you know your friend well and her food allergy because you have a close, personal relationship with your friend. The same can be true of our relationship with God as we get to know God personally. Over time, we can discern and understand, through wisdom, what is and what isn't God's will.

Sometimes God's will is evident because the matter is extremely evident; you can easily discern the right decision and God's will. But, there are many times when the course and direction aren't as clear, and you struggle with identifying God's will. In these times, you must lean deeply on your relationship with God, as well as those in your circle who also know and trust God to help you discern the path and direction of God's will.

I have had many struggles involving heavy discernment in my life concerning relationships, career, conversation content, and even physical moves from one state to another. Even though I have a personal relationship with God, there are times when discerning God's will is challenging. I am thankful in those times for the wise sages in my life who help light my path and embody the wisdom of the psalmist:

> *Your word is a lamp to my feet and a light to my path.*
>
> **Psalm 119:105 (NRSV)**

I wish I had some super-spiritual strategy that would make discernment easier, like praying each day at a specific time or making sure to read the Bible every year from Genesis to Revelation. But even practicing these disciplines doesn't prevent the times of uncertainty from entering your mind. I know there are seasons when you will pray and read the Bible, and you will still miss the mark in discerning God's will. On those occasions, don't judge yourself. Instead, embrace God's grace, dust yourself off, and faithfully live to try again.

Jesus goes on to say in Matthew 6:10, "on Earth as it is in Heaven." The Heaven imagery is kingdom-talk about Jesus wanting to see Heaven on Earth.

I know we covered God's Kingdom in the previous chapter, but allow me to mention an additional thought on the subject. Growing up, I learned the phrase, "my little piece of Heaven." Typically, someone had purchased land and built their dream home, and to them, it was their "little piece of Heaven." They were living their dream in their oasis.

Jesus wants us all to experience a piece of Heaven on Earth. We could all use a little more Heaven on Earth in the midst of the hardships we face daily. Some years ago, Dr. Martin Luther King, Jr., captured Jesus' image of Heaven on Earth and what it would mean for all people to live by God's will in his famous *I Have a Dream* speech.

On a hot summer day in August 1963, Dr. King prophetically proclaimed:

*And when we allow freedom to ring, when we let*
*it ring from every village and hamlet, from every*
*state and city, we will be able to speed up that day*
*when all of God's children – black men and white*
*men, Jews and Gentiles, Catholics and Protestants*
*– will be able to join hands and to sing in the words*
*of the old Negro spiritual, "Free at last, free at*
*last; thank God Almighty, we are free at last."* [29]

Dr. King dreamed of the day when the Earth would look like heaven. We pray and hope for the day when his dream comes true, and all the world resembles God's Kingdom.

Whenever we pray, "Your will be done, on Earth as it is in Heaven," we are literally asking for Heaven to come to Earth. We pray like Jesus and dream like Dr. King of a whole new world and a whole new Earth. Perhaps you get a euphoric feeling when you think about this new world and wish you could always be inspired this way. However, at other times, we also experience the tension of living God's will as Jesus did in the Garden of Gethsemane.

Remember Jesus' words:

*My Father, if it is possible, let this cup pass*
*from me; yet not what I want but what you want.*

**Matthew 26:39 (NRSV)**

---

[29] James Washington, ed. *A Testament of Hope: The Essential Writings and Speeches of Martin Luther King, Jr.* (San Francisco, Harper, 1986), 217-220.

Jesus' words of surrender to God's will exemplify how living it can be freeing but also challenging when we are called to suffering or sacrifice. Releasing our own will to embrace God's will is the quintessential Lent sacrifice as we prepare ourselves for Easter. Earth looks a little more like Heaven whenever we accept God's will, even if following it isn't easy.

I am thankful that Jesus surrendered to God's will in the Garden of Gethsemane because it cleared the path to Easter. This Lent, remember that God's will is available for you. If you are willing to surrender and follow God's way – not your own – God's direction for your life can become apparent.

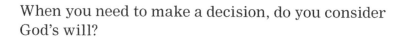
# Questions:

When you need to make a decision, do you consider God's will?

Is discerning God's will easy or difficult for you?

How do you discern God's will in your life?

When you are walking in God's will for your life, what are some of the tangible signs of confirmation you have seen?

What would surrendering to God's will this Lenten season look like for you? What would it take for you to surrender?

Like Jesus in the Garden of Gethsemane, what tensions are you experiencing when trying to follow God's will for your life?

How can you make Earth look a little more like Heaven?

## CHAPTER SIX
# Daily Bread

*Bread of heaven, bread of heaven,*
*Feed me till I want no more.*[30]

**Give us this day our daily bread.**

**Matthew 6:11 (NRSV)**

I admit, this verse is one of my favorite verses
in the Bible. A question to consider is, "What type of
bread was Jesus referring to in Matthew's recitation
of the Lord's Prayer?" Consider the following two
answers. One type of bread is bread for today only, *I*
immediate nourishment. The second type of bread is
symbolic, eschatological; this speaks to what is hoped
I FUTURE
for and desired in the future. A working definition of
eschatological is a "Study of the 'last things' or the end
of the world."[31] After reflecting on the life and times of
Jesus, I believe Jesus was referencing both versions of

---

[30]  Michael Hawn. *History of Hymns:"Guide Me, O Thou Great Jehovah"* Discipleship
Ministries. https://www.umcdiscipleship.org/resources/history-of-hymns-guide-me-o-
thou-great-jehovah. (2015, March 12) Accessed October 12, 2021.

[31]  Donald K. McKim. *The Westminister Dictionary of Theological Terms.* (Louisville, Kentucky:
Westminister John Knox Press, 2014), 105-106.

bread: bread that provides immediate nourishment as well as nourishment for the future.

Jesus petitioned God and taught his disciples to ask for daily bread, that is, enough bread to fulfill their needs for that day. This was an act of faith because he didn't ask for a bread manufacturing company or truck filled with bread to last an entire year. Just enough bread for today.

This clause in the Lord's Prayer challenges us to have faith and trust God to provide our "daily bread;" in other words, we can trust God for resources, love, generosity, and protection each day. Jesus completely trusted God to protect and keep him, and through faith, he believed. It would have been easy for Jesus to ask God to provide enough bread to last a year and then for Jesus to place his faith on autopilot. Instead, Jesus asked for enough bread to last one day.

When you pray, do you ask God for bread for one day, or do you ask God for enough bread to last the entire year? However you answer this question, it isn't about judgment, but rather to help clarify your faith and evaluate if you trust God to give you everything you need each day.

Lent is all about trusting that God will keep you and supply your needs, even in the wilderness or the Garden of Gethsemane. In the difficult moments of our lives, we need faith the most. The Lord's Prayer is more than words and phrases coordinated together; it is a statement of faith that is lived out through our actions as we trust God to answer our prayer.

It is common to fill our physical or online shopping carts with more than we need; sometimes, we order excess, just in case. But what would it look like this Lent to trust God each day for only the amount you need for that day, then when you get up the next day – like the dew on the grass – more of what you need will be available? If we aren't careful, when we pray this part of the Lord's Prayer, we can prioritize quantity over quality, and instead of asking God for enough bread for today, we ask God for enough bread to last a lifetime.

The bread Jesus refers to in the text is more than physical bread. The hymn "Guide Me, O Thou Great Jehovah" by Methodist minister and hymn writer William Williams beautifully glorifies Matthew 6:11:

> *Guide me, O thou great Jehovah,*
> *Pilgrim through this barren land.*
> *I am weak, but thou art mighty;*
> *Hold me with thy powerful hand.*
> *Bread of Heaven, bread of Heaven,*
> *Feed me till I want no more.*[32]

This hymn asks God for "Bread of Heaven" and to "feed me till I want no more." The imagery and passion

---

[32] Michael Hawn. *History of Hymns:"Guide Me, O Thou Great Jehovah"* Discipleship Ministries. https://www.umcdiscipleship.org/resources/history-of-hymns-guide-me-o-thou-great-jehovah. (2015, March 12) Accessed October 12, 2021.

of these well-penned words leap from the page, resonate in the atmosphere through singing voices, and affirm our faith in God Almighty, our Creator, and Provider of every need. Even if you didn't know this great hymn of the church, you may have experienced the words of the hymn in your own journey and wanted God to feed and provide for you so that you always have enough. As you are praying this Lent, ask God to fill you up and provide for you that which can only be supplied from the storerooms of Heaven. Then you will not only be praying and singing this great hymn of the church, you will also be living it.

"Give us this day" is a simple yet profound request. It is straightforward in that it lists the timetable and delivery day in a certain way. It is profound because it requires us to trust that we only need to ask for enough to cover our daily needs, not some large quantity of bread at one time to store in case the bread supply runs out.

Jesus' request is more about faith than bread and teaches us that, through faith, we can ask God for a daily supply, knowing we don't need to anxiously store up love, mercy, grace, favor, forgiveness, wholeness, or peace for an unknown time in the future. We can freely give to others and trust God will replenish our supply daily.

When was the last time you had an experience where you had to trust God completely and trust God for every resource you needed? Do you remember how you felt or what you were thinking? Chances are, you were nervous, anxious, and concerned because you weren't sure God would come through, and you questioned God's word. Instead of staying in the place of trust, you decided to "help" God. So, you stored God's blessings, not for good conservation practices for the future but because of a deficit of faith in the now.

I once preached a sermon about Jesus' type of faith and cautioned the listeners about having a faith that doesn't fully trust God and attempts to store blessings "just in case." The concern is not about conservation, preserving, or saving – because God doesn't mind us preparing for the future – but about fully trusting God in the present, knowing that God will meet our needs in the future. This "just-in-case faith" doesn't fully allow you to lean and depend on God.

During Lent, I invite you to let God grow your faith as you work on eliminating your "just-in-case" storage practices and by asking and trusting God for daily bread. One of my favorite scriptures that illustrates this point is also found in Mathew's Gospel:

> *Therefore, I say to you, don't worry about your life, what you'll eat or what you'll drink, or about your body, what you'll wear. Isn't life more than food and the body more than clothes? Look at the birds in the sky. They don't sow seed or harvest grain or gather crops into barns.*

*Yet your heavenly Father feeds them. Aren't you worth much more than they are? Who among you by worrying can add a single moment to your life?*

**Matthew 6:25-27 (CEB)**

The second type of bread Jesus was referring to is eschatological bread, which is bread for the future beyond today's needs. When we pray with an eschatological faith for daily bread, we are not only praying for bread today, but we are also praying for bread for the generations and centuries to come. Eschatology looks beyond now into the future. We believe that the future will be even better through faith because the God of time and history is already there. Wherever God is, there is more than enough.

During church, the elders in the community that raised me would make a request of God through prayer during church, "God bless the unborn generations." This prayer was asking God, through eschatological faith, to bless future generations, now and forever. Just as we must have faith to trust God for daily bread, we must also have faith and trust God to provide bread for future generations.

Whenever you pray about your family, community, nation, or world, you are praying in a form of eschatological faith because you believe God can provide for you now and for your future. This type of prayer is powerful because you are declaring and decreeing God's blessings over a time that hasn't yet arrived, precisely what Jesus did in praying the Lord's Prayer. Jesus prayed that we would have bread today and tomorrow and fully trust in God's provision.

# Questions:

What are examples of daily bread?

Have you ever struggled in your faith, and instead of trusting God for daily bread, you asked God to supply you with bread for a lifetime?

What would it look like this Lent to trust God each day for the exact amount you need and know when you arise the next day, like the dew on the grass, more of what you need will be available?

As you think about eschatological faith, what do you need to ask God to supply in your future?

Are you able to make a shift in faith to trust God for today and tomorrow, even when the environment around you shows the complete opposite from your faith?

*To Let go of the past.*
*a journey,*
*setting self free,*
*pardon, record of the wrong.*

# CHAPTER SEVEN

# Forgiveness

*Lord, I want to be a Christian in my heart,*
*Lord, I want to be more loving in my heart,*
*Lord, I want to be more holy in my heart,*
*Lord, I want to be like Jesus in my heart.*[33]

**And forgive us our debts, as we also have**
**forgiven our debtors.**
**Matthew 6:12 (NRSV)**

Admittedly, I did not look forward to writing this chapter because I knew I would have to address my own tension with receiving and offering forgiveness in my life. Perhaps that sounds strange to you, considering I am a pastor and have worked in the local church for many years. One might assume receiving and offering forgiveness comes easy to me, but this is not true. It is a daily mountain to climb for me.

Matthew 6:12 is a specific, unambiguous request to God: "And forgive us our debts as we also have forgiven our debtors" Matthew 6:12 (NRSV). I like the Common English Bible translation:

---

[33] Afro-American Spiritual. "Lord, I Want to Be a Christian" The United Methodist Hymnal, 1989, p. 402-403.

*Forgive us for the ways we have wronged you, just
as we also forgive those who have wronged us.*

**Matthew 6:12 (CEB)**

Both translations begin by asking God to forgive *us*
our debts, or ways we have wronged others. In this bold
prayer request, we humbly present ourselves to God,
acknowledging we have been out of line and did not live
our lives or act in a way aligned with God's will.

Think about the last time you hurt someone else
in word or deed. You didn't have to think but a second
or two before realizing what you did was wrong. Was
it hard to admit it to yourself? Was it hard to admit it
to the person you hurt? The likely answer is yes. Being
able to recognize when we are wrong is the spiritual
discipline of self-awareness and accountability. In
the Lord's Prayer, Jesus teaches us, when we are
accountable to God, we are also accountable to others;
therefore, forgiveness is the healthiest option.

Whenever we focus on forgiveness, it is necessary
to talk about repentance. *Repentance* is a powerful
word. To repent means I am sorry for what I did, and I
am turning away from my error and going in the opposite
direction. When we ask God for forgiveness, we are taking
responsibility for our actions and committing to go in a
different direction, God's direction.

During Lent, consider pausing just for a moment
each day to think about the forgiveness you need.

If you take that moment and nothing comes to your consciousness, I encourage you to stay with it for a bit longer. The Apostle Paul reminded us in Philippians about the daily process of making the mark:

> *Not that I have already obtained this or have already reached the goal, but I press on to make it my own because Christ Jesus has made me his own.*
> **Philippians 3:12 (NRSV)**

Even when we consciously try to do everything the right way – to love everyone abundantly, refrain from judging or hating others – we still fall short of the goal. To forgive and love all people wholeheartedly is a dream and hope that will only be perfected in Heaven. While we live on Earth, at best we are imperfect.

To ask God for forgiveness is a sign of humility because it is an acknowledgment that God is God, and we are not; it is an acknowledgment that God's grace is available for all people, and through the sacrifice of Jesus on the cross, the debt for our sins has been paid.

The song *Standing in the Need,* written by pastor and singer/songwriter John P. Kee, narrates the journey of a person who realizes they need prayer and need God. Whenever we pray the Lord's Prayer, we are deeply concerned about the world's needs, but we are also focusing on ourselves and our personal relationship with God. In essence, whenever we pray the Lord's

Prayer, we are saying, "God, I am in need of prayer."

The good news is when we ask God for forgiveness, God hears and answers. When I say God hears you and answers, that means wherever you are in life when you reach out and call on God for forgiveness, the answer is always a resounding "Yes!"

Unfortunately, when some people pray for forgiveness, they feel that God does not hear or answer them because of their life circumstances or because they feel undeserving of God's mercy. I have experienced moments in my own life when I didn't feel close to God or felt God didn't hear me because of my sin. I now know God was always with me and will always be with me despite my hangups and setbacks. I realize this was a limited view of God and God's love. God's love is all-surpassing, all-encompassing, all-merciful.

Remember Paul's encouragement in Romans:

> *For I am convinced that neither death, nor life, nor angels, nor rulers, nor things present, nor things to come, nor powers, nor height, nor depth, nor anything else in all creation, will be able to separate us from the love of God in Christ Jesus our Lord.*
>
> **Romans 8:38-39 (NRSV)**

The sequence of the forgiveness request in the Lord's Prayer is essential to understand. God first forgives our sins, and second, we forgive the sins people have committed against us. Sounds easy, right? It's not so easy in practice. I struggle not only with asking for and receiving God's forgiveness for my transgressions, but I also struggle to forgive others of the wrongs they have committed against me. Something tells me I am not the only person with this struggle.

Two inspiring examples of persons living forgiveness in modern times are Nelson Mandela and the family members whose loved ones were killed by Dylann Roof while attending Bible study at their church in Charleston, South Carolina.

Nelson Mandela was convicted of sabotage and sentenced to life in prison, and ultimately, a corrupt and racist government took 27 years of his life. He was the victim of a racist government and country towards his people. He endured hardship, false accusations, unequal treatment, isolation, and imprisonment as an innocent man. Whenever we hear Nelson Mandela's story, there is a quick gloss over of the 27 years he spent in prison, and narrators focus on the years and legacy he left as the president of South Africa.

*From Prison to President* is the most popular narrative of Mandela's life. As great of an accomplishment as it was, the 27 years he spent in prison weren't tranquil. He recounted the day he was arrested in front of his children:

*It isn't pleasant to be arrested in front of one's children, even though one knows that what one is doing is right...they simply see their father being taken away by the white authorities without an explanation.* [34]

For 27 years, he experienced life away from his children, his family, and his community. Mandela described his confinement during part of his imprisonment:

*I was assigned a cell at the head of the corridor. It overlooked the courtyard and had a small eye-level window. I could walk the length of my cell in three paces. When I lay down, I could feel the wall with my feet, and my head grazed the concrete at the other side.* [35]

We celebrate the time that Mandela spent as the President of South Africa and living in conditions in stark contrast to the prison cell that confined his body. Still, we must not forget the 27 years of confinement that tried to take his hope and power of forgiveness. Even with harsh and unfathomable conditions, his love for his family, community, nation, and justice endured. Mandela represented the unquenchable passion of fire when you fight for justice and equality for all people.

Although I don't know what was in Mandela's

---

[34]  Nelson Mandela. *Long Walk to Freedom*. (New York: Little, Brown and Company, 1995), 199.

[35]  Ibid., 384.

heart, a statement he wrote towards the end of his autobiography captures the depth of the Lord's Prayer words "as we also have forgiven our debtors" Matthew 6:12 (NRSV).

His statement in a news conference shortly after his release from prison embodies forgiveness:

> *I ended by opening my arms to all South Africans of goodwill and good intentions, saying that 'no man or woman who has abandoned apartheid will be excluded from our movement toward a nonracial, united democratic South Africa based on one-person one-vote on a common voters' roll.' That was the ANC's mission, the goal that I had always kept before me during the many lonely years in prison, the goal that I would work toward during the remaining years of my life. It was the dream I cherished when I entered prison at the age of forty-four, but I was no longer a young man, I was seventy-one, and I could not afford to waste any time.*[36]

Mandela's reflection on moving beyond the past and building a coalition advocating justice for all was rightly placed in a chapter entitled "Freedom." Mandela was right. We can't afford to waste any time. Withholding forgiveness is a waste of time, and the longer we choose not to forgive, the more time we waste. I hope this

---

36  Ibid., 570.

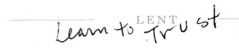

Lent you surrender your unforgiveness to God and begin living your life in the bright and warm light of forgiveness, no longer settling for the confinement of past hurt and pain that you and so many others have endured. This Lent, choose freedom.

Another poignant example of forgiveness shines through one of the most horrific American domestic terrorist events in modern-day history. On June 17, 2015, Dylann Roof walked into Mother Emanuel African Methodist Episcopal Church in Charleston, South Carolina. After being welcomed by the pastor and parishioners and listening through the entire Bible study, he opened fire on the participants. He shot and killed nine people in cold blood: the Rev. Sharonda Coleman-Singleton; Cynthia Hurd; Susie Jackson; Ethel Lee Lance; the Rev. Depayne Middleton-Doctor; Tywanza Sanders; the Rev. Daniel Simmons, Sr., Rev. Myra Thompson, and the church's pastor, the Rev. Clementa Pinckney. Then-President Barack Obama gave a memorial eulogy for Rev. Pinckney and ended by singing the words of the hymn "Amazing Grace."

The world was dismayed and shocked and could not believe a domestic terrorist attack of that magnitude was possible, especially to be committed on the sacred and holy ground of a church building while parishioners were innocently studying the Word of God. A *Washington Post* article carried the

*reconciled*

title, "'I forgive you.' Relatives of the Charleston church shooting victims address Dylann Roof," the story of family members of the slain shared their journey of forgiveness.[37] The news article reported:

> **The relatives of people slain inside the historic African American church in Charleston, S.C., earlier this week were able to speak directly to the accused gunman Friday at his first court appearance. One by one, those who chose to speak at a bond hearing did not turn to anger. Instead, while he remained impassive, they offered him forgiveness and said they were praying for his soul, even as they described the pain of their losses.[38]**

The family members of the slain victims did the seemingly impossible: they forgave a person who brutally murdered their loved ones during a church prayer meeting. There were those who read this account, and in their own pain of loss and grief wondered, *How could these family members forgive so soon and so absolutely?*

Because of the injustices and hurt done to us individually and collectively, we all question how forgiveness can be possible from time to time. Still, I

---

37 Mark Berman. (2015, June 19). 'I forgive you.' Relatives of Charleston church shooting victims address Dylann Roof. *The Washington Post.* https://www.washingtonpost.com/news/post-nation/wp/2015/06/19/i-forgive-you-relatives-of-charleston-church-victims-address-dylann-roof/.

38 Ibid.

believe the short, most plausible answer is God. The article recorded that the families forgave Dylann Roof at his first court appearance, not when he had been convicted and sentenced. The families of the slain actually forgave him shortly after he had committed the horrible act, and then they prayed for his soul. There is no timetable on forgiveness and how long it takes one to forgive. Only God knows. If you are struggling with forgiveness, you are not alone because a great majority of people in the world are struggling with you. Please don't place the pressure of a forgiveness goal or timeline on yourself, but each day open your heart to God to give you the strength and the willingness to forgive.

Forgiving others, in general, is challenging, and forgiving people when they commit horrible atrocities against the most vulnerable and innocent in our society is even more difficult. Whether it is Nelson Mandela arriving at a place of forgiveness for those who stole decades of his life, preventing him from being with his young children in the most precious years of their lives, or whether it is family members offering forgiveness after their loved ones were brutally murdered while worshiping in their church, time and time again, forgiving others seems next to impossible. I believe forgiveness is only possible when we fully receive God's grace and fully offer God's grace to others. There is no middle ground to grace. Either it is grace, or it is not. I

lean on the side of grace.

We have to ask ourselves, "If Jesus can forgive those who were crucifying him, can I forgive those who have harmed me?" The quick answer is yes, but the more accurate answer is, "It's a process." When Jesus said these words about forgiving others, I don't believe he thought it was a three-step plan, and then all would be well in love and war. No. Jesus knew it would take some of us a lifetime to forgive, and for some, it may never happen on this side of glory.

I am not naive enough to think that a few paragraphs in this chapter will cause you to put the book down and immediately receive God's forgiveness or instantly offer God's forgiveness to someone else. I do believe, however, this book and chapter can be part of your forgiveness journey and process.

# Questions:

What is forgiveness to you?

What are areas of your life in need of forgiveness?

*Willingness to forgive someone for Prayer*

*Strength*

What does communal forgiveness look like for acts of discrimination towards groups of people (i.e., Native Americans, African Americans, Latin Americans and Asian Americans)?

*642- 642AM Prayer line 667 770 536*

*971565 #*

Can you think of examples you've seen where people who have been hurt or mistreated by others offer forgiveness to their perpetrators? How did you feel about their decision to forgive?

This Lent, is God asking you to forgive someone who wronged you? What would it take for you to offer forgiveness to them?

CHAPTER EIGHT

# Fighting Temptation and Deliverance

*Almighty God, your blessed Son was led*
*by the Spirit to be tempted by Satan.*
*Come quickly to help us who are assaulted*
*by many temptations.*
*And, as you know the weakness of each of us,*
*let each one find you mighty to save;*
*through Jesus Christ your Son, our Lord. Amen.*[39]

**And do not bring us to the time of trial, but**
**rescue us from the evil one.**

**Matthew 6:13 (NRSV)**

Is God in the business of tempting humanity? It
is hard for me to believe God has nothing better to do
than to spend days, weeks, months, and years setting up
temptation traps for people on Earth. When we review
the verse, "And do not bring us to the time of trial," it is
clear that temptation is part of the human experience,
but the source of it isn't God. To be human is to live each
day experiencing some form of temptation. Temptation
is an equal opportunity employer for persons of all
ages. Every person is tempted, and every person falls to

---

[39] *The United Methodist Book of Worship.* "Lent" (Nashville: The United Methodist
Publishing House, 1992), 333.

temptation from time to time. Resisting temptation does not get easier with age. The nature of the temptations may change, but we will always be tempted by something.

*Temptation* is having a desire or need for something that may or may not be good for you. When the word *temptation* is written or said, we may quickly assume it refers to something negative or, for instance, being tempted by something or someone that isn't good. This ideology isn't completely true because there are temptations to which yielding can be beneficial.

For example, during Lent, you may be *tempted* to try fasting for the first time because you have witnessed how others' faith deepened and their relationships with God grew as they practiced the spiritual discipline of fasting. Maybe you experienced a persistent nudging in your spirit to reach out to someone you haven't talked to in a while. Or, after twenty-five years in the same career, perhaps you are tempted to return to school and follow a different road map or get a new certification in a completely different career because you feel God wants you to do a new thing. Obviously, these describe healthy temptations, but there are plenty of destructive temptations.

Of course, I could fill a couple of hundred pages with just a tiny fraction of the negative temptations we face daily, but we all know what those temptations are and understand the specific temptations we struggle with personally. I have always taught that temptation is contextual and designed individually for you; that is why it is your temptation. This perspective also keeps me from looking down on others who fall to a particular temptation that I wouldn't necessarily fall to because I know my temptations are contextual.

Rather than list a series of temptations, I would instead ask a question: Are you aware of the temptations in your life, and are you willing to surrender to God to help you through each and every temptation?

Even Jesus was tempted, and I believe it is important to note that when Jesus was tempted, God and the angels were always there to strengthen and protect him. I am not saying that we will always pass with flying colors like Jesus, but we need to remember that, in each temptation, we are never alone because God is with us.

When Jesus' time of temptation ended, the text says:

> *Then the devil left him, and suddenly angels came and waited on him.*
>
> **Matthew 4:11 (NRSV)**

Although the text says, "suddenly angels came," I believe the angels never left him. I think they were with him every step of the way. Jesus' body was tempted, his power was tempted, and his relationship with God was tempted, yet he stood the test because he willfully surrendered to God's love and grace.

Like Jesus, you won't have to look for temptation during this Lenten season; it will find you.

In the most trying moments, will you fully surrender to God, or will you try to win the battle yourself? If you answer that you will try to win by your own means, chances are you will lose every time because your temptations are contextual. Your temptations will know precisely how to get you when you are frustrated, ego-tripping, angry, tired, or feeling defeated.

Surrendering is what the second half of the verse is talking about:

> *...rescue us from the evil one.*
>
> **Matthew 6:13 (NRSV)**

To be rescued, we must surrender and accept that God is greater than our circumstances, actively working to make a difference in our lives.

I have placed a daily prayer of protection on a mirror in my home that I see multiple times a day. I have gotten into a habit of praying the prayer even on days when my faith is low or I am tired and don't feel like making the prayer of confession. On those days when I am the weakest, and my faith is the lowest, those are the days when the prayer of confession makes the most difference in my life because I am unable to fight for myself, and I completely surrender to God.

Similar to the journey of forgiveness, the journey

of surrendering is not a walk in the park. It is an intentional, daily practice of letting go and trusting that God is in control.

New Testament scholar M. Eugene Boring wrote the following reflection of this verse on temptation in his commentary on the Gospel of Matthew:

> *Although initially primarily eschatological, the petition for deliverance from the final testing and the evil one also has a present dimension. The 'ordinary' testings and temptations are seen not as pretty peccadilloes but as manifestations of the ultimate power of evil. The disciple is instructed not to take them lightly, but to see them as a threat to faith and to pray for God's deliverance from them.*[40]

The severe warning Jesus gave about temptation to his followers two thousand years ago is still real and relevant today. As modern-day believers, every temptation must be taken seriously and approached with caution. Your life matters and the enemy will do everything within the enemy's power to derail, distract, delay, or detour you from your purpose and God's plan for your life. Remember, temptation is serious and God is always willing and available to rescue you. Try living a life of surrender and receive God's protection from and during every temptation.

---

[40] M. Eugene Boring. *The New Interpreter's Bible*, Vol VIII. "The Gospel of Matthew" (Nashville: Abingdon Press, 1995), 205.

# Questions:

Do you believe God is the source of our negative temptations?

Do you believe Jesus was tempted in the wilderness? If so, how was he able to overcome the temptations?

Are you aware of the temptations in your life, and are you willing to surrender to God to help you through every temptation?

This Lent, are you willing to surrender to God to overcome temptations in your life?

# CHAPTER NINE
# Your Personal Doxology

*To God be the Glory for the things [God] has done.*[41]

**For thine is the kingdom, and the power, and the glory, for ever. Amen.**

**Matthew 6:13b (KJV)**

A great definition of *doxology* is:

**A form of praise to God..."**[42]

Some versions of Matthew 6:13 end with the following doxology:

**For thine is the kingdom, and the power, and the glory, for ever. Amen.**

**Matthew 6:13b (KJV)**

New Testament scholar M. Eugene Boring, referenced in the previous chapter, wrote this about the Lord's Prayer doxology:

---

[41] Crouch, Andrae. "My Tribute." The United Methodist Hymnal, 1989, p. 99.

[42] Donald K. McKim. *The Westminister Dictionary of Theological Terms.* (Louisville, Kentucky: Westminister John Knox Press, 2014), 95.

*The manuscript tradition contains ten different endings to the Lord's Prayer, testifying to its frequent use and adoption in the life of the church.*[43]

Because of different translations and interpretations, there may be several endings to the Lord's Prayer in the biblical text throughout history. This historical fact is not meant to cause you to question your faith or the validity of the Bible, but it is intended to help you understand the Bible from a spiritual and historical point of view.

New Testament scholar John Yieh also confirmed the multiple doxologies for the Lord's Prayer and their use throughout the Christian world:

*As witnessed in ancient manuscripts, the concluding doxology found in many modern versions and translation of the Lord's Prayer is a later addition. As an important development of the church's liturgy, nonetheless, this triple strophic form of doxology lifts our perspectives from earthly human concerns upward to God our Heavenly Father with the confession of faith, love, and hope for God's Kingdom, power, and glory to be manifested now and forever.*[44]

Although the doxology was added later, it is a historical way of ending the Lord's Prayer for people

---

43  Ibid., 205.

44  John Yieh. The New Interpreter's Dictionary of the Bible. Vol III. "Lord's Prayer" (Nashville: Abingdon Press, 2008), 690-695.

worldwide. The doxology recognizes God alone as the deity over the earth – "thine is the kingdom" – and acknowledges God's power and glory. This particular doxology seals God's reign over all the Earth as God and Creator with the final phrase, "for ever. Amen." It is a doxology filled with honor and references God as having all power and glory.

In the Christian faith, if we are not careful, we can sing beautiful anthems and hymns and recite responsive readings, creeds, and doxologies out of tradition and miss the words' meanings and the opportunity for a spiritual transformation.

Admittedly, this has often happened to me. Every Sunday, I participate in multiple worship experiences. I have to remind myself that even though this is my third worship experience of the day, it is still the first worship experience for those physically sitting in the congregation and those watching online. In these moments of self-awareness, after reflecting on the doxology in Matthew's Gospel, I am reminded of God's great glory and power and that, even in my finite ability, I am covered and protected by God Almighty. I thank God for those moments of self and spiritual awareness and helping me to see beyond the tradition of church and experience the power of God's transformative work in my life.

Take a moment to say the doxology out loud and allow it to resonate in your soul: "For thine is the kingdom, and the power, and the glory, for ever. Amen." What did you hear and feel?

We are fortunate that the redactors added the doxology because it is entirely possible to pray, and before the prayer ends, forget that this is all about God. The doxology is like a fail-safe in our spiritual lives that reminds us when we communicate with God through prayer, the conversation begins and ends with God.

In the third chapter, we talked about the importance of using inclusive language for God. I challenged you to consider how we have over-indexed male pronouns for God and that God is a spirit, meaning God doesn't have a bodily form that is male or female. I know this isn't an easy task or even an easy concept to grasp, especially if you were not raised in a tradition that offered you that theological freedom.

What if you permitted yourself to release God from the bondage of your pronouns? What if you also allowed yourself to create your own personal, powerful ending of Matthew 6:13 to the Lord's Prayer? Here are a few steps to consider:

- Read the Lord's Prayer out loud several times in the version you prefer.

- Record yourself reading the Lord's Prayer aloud, and then play it back several times to hear the words audibly.

- Take a moment to think about your relationship with God and what God means to you.

- Once you have thought about your relationship with God, begin drafting a few words and phrases that will be the content of your doxology. Some of the expressions might be: "awesome God; forgiving God; wise and all-knowing, merciful, and kind God."

- Finally, arrange your words and phrases in the sequence that speaks to you. Once your doxology is complete, try saying the entire Lord's Prayer and end with the doxology version you wrote.

I hope this exercise is freeing for you and allows you to receive the Lord's Prayer in a new and different way.

# CONCLUSION
# Transformation

Now that we have taken our journey through
the Lord's Prayer, you have a unique opportunity to
follow the instructions that Jesus gave to his disciples
and discover this transformative way of praying,
even if you have been praying the Lord's Prayer for
years. This Lenten season, I hope you do not live out
the spiritual disciplines through rote memory and
mandatory performances of spirituality. Rather, I
encourage you to look deeply within, and through your
prayer conversations with God, trust that the spiritual
disciplines you practice are more than traditions but acts
of transformation through the power of the Holy Spirit.

The Lord's Prayer is more than words on a page
or one of the first prayers you learned as a child. It is a
prayer of illumination that speaks through the ages to
all the ages, calling Jesus' followers to pray differently.
It was, and is, a renewal of the spiritual discipline of
prayer and confession.

During Lent, I challenge you to engage the Lord's
Prayer differently and consider the following approaches:

- Say the Lord's Prayer within your inner consciousness and sense what God is saying to you.

- Say the Lord's Prayer out loud and consider what you hear audibly through the prayer.

- Dare to live the Lord's Prayer by surrendering to God's will for your life and trusting God's grace is always with you.

As you are going through various spiritual disciplines, in particular those disciplines that call for you to subtract something from your life, perhaps when it comes to the spiritual discipline of prayer, try adding. Add being focused on what God is saying to you personally and what God is saying to the world. Add that God is holy, and wherever God is, you are standing on holy ground. Add a commitment to live in such a way that the Earth will look a little more like Heaven because you exist, and be diligent in giving your time and life away for good causes. Add praying for bread for today and bread for unborn generations. Finally, add receiving and giving forgiveness and overcoming temptations by yielding to God daily.

These additions are not easy and will take more than commitment. They will take surrender. So often on the spiritual journey, we think God wants us to do something, but more so, God wants us to simply be and allow God to be God in our lives and experiences. One of the best ways to surrender is to come to God humbly in prayer and confess that we have not fully lived up to the call or purpose for our lives. In the Communion liturgy in my faith tradition, we pray the following *Prayer of Confession and Pardon:*[45]

> *Merciful God,*
> *We confess that we have not loved you with our*
> *   whole heart.*
> *We have failed to be an obedient church.*
> *We have not done your will,*
> *We have broken your law*
> *We have rebelled against your love,*
> *We have not loved our neighbors,*
> *And we have not heard the cry of the needy.*
> *Forgive us, we pray.*
> *Free us for joyful obedience,*
> *Through Jesus Christ our Lord. Amen.*

Although I have prayed this Prayer of Confession over the years, I am not quite sure that I always received and understood the prayer or my confession. I now understand and receive it. For me today, the Prayer of Confession means to stand in the presence of an all-loving, all-forgiving God and – despite my past, present, or future – to hear God say, "You are completely forgiven."

My hope for you during this Lenten season is that, through the Lord's Prayer, you will receive God's

---

45 "A Service of Word and Table I," Copyright © 1972, The Methodist Publishing House; Copyright © 1980, 1985, 1989, 1992 UMPH.

complete forgiveness and be freed into new life and the power of Easter. I also pray that you will abundantly offer forgiveness and grace to others and allow God's power to transform you.

As we close this Lenten journey and live knowing the ultimate victory comes through the Easter Resurrection story, I offer you this final doxology I composed. I can't wait for you to write your own personal doxology and share it with the world, but for now, my doxology will have to do:

> *To God be the Glory, and may God's grace,*
> *favor, and love be with you always and forever.*
> *Amen.*

# Join Olu Brown

for Advent 2022

marketsquarebooks.com

# More Titles
## from Market Square Books

2022 Lenten Study
**Journey to Transformation**
Bishop Sharma Lewis

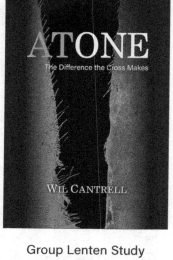

Group Lenten Study
**ATONE**
The Difference the Cross Makes

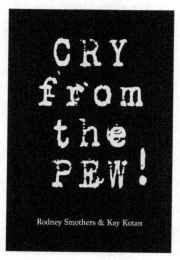

**Cry from the Pew!**
Rodney Smothers
& Kay Kotan

**A New Kind**
of Venture Leader
Olu Brown

# Recent Studies

from Market Square Books

marketsquarebooks.com

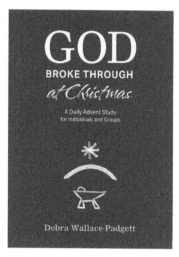

## God Broke Through
## at Christmas

Bishop Debra Wallace-Padgett

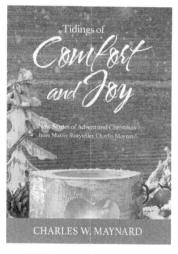

## Tidings of Comfort
## and Joy

Charles W. Maynard

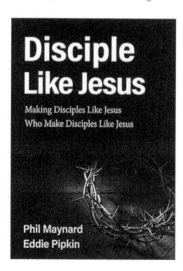

## Disciple Like Jesus

Making Disciples Like Jesus Who Make Disciples Like Jesus

Phil Maynard & Eddie Pipkin

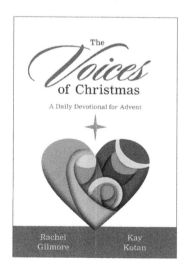

## Voices of Christmas

A Daily Devotional for Advent

Kay Kotan & Rachel Gilmore

# Great Study Books

## for your small group or class

marketsquarebooks.com

**Growing the
Post-Pandemic Church**

Rebekah Simon-Peter

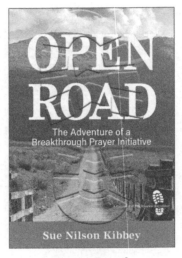

**Open Road**
**The Adenture of Breakthrough Prayer**

Sue Nilson Kibbey

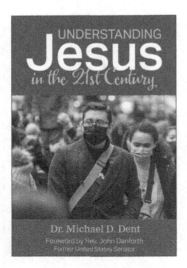

**Understanding Jesus
in the 21st Century**

Dr. Michael D. Dent

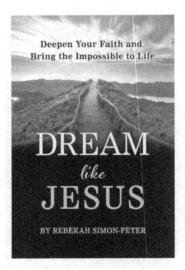

**Dream Like Jesus**

Deepen Your Faith and Bring
the Impossible to Life

Bread chp6
Needs of bread
- Substance meant to survive
Bread cloth, shelter
Bread - all encompassing bread

evolving
The word Jesus spoke: physical
+
spiritual

Made in United States
North Haven, CT
02 March 2022